TAKE CONTROL OF YOUR LIFE

A GUIDE TO ACHIEVING SELF-MASTERY AND HAPPINESS

ROBERT O. OWOLABI, M.Eng.

Bob and Bob Publishing
Gaithersburg, Maryland, U.S.A.

Copyright © 2001 Robert O. Owolabi

First Printing December 2001
All Rights Reserved
Published by:
Bob & Bob Publishing
Post Office Box 10246
Gaithersburg, MD 20898-0246 U.S.A.
http://www.bobandbob.com
e-mail: bobandbobinc@aol.com

No part of this book may be reproduced or transmitted in any form or by any means, electronic, mechanical, including photocopying, recording, or by any information storage and retrieval system, except in the case of reviews, without the express written permission of the publisher, except where permitted by law.

Cover Design by Stacey L. King, Crystal Moon Design

Library Of Congress Publisher's Cataloging-in-Publication

Library of Congress Card Number: 2001117910

ISBN: 0-9666450-1-4

Printed by: Signature Book Printing, Inc.
 Gaithersburg, MD, USA

PRINTED IN THE UNITED STATES OF AMERICA
05 04 03 02 01   10 9 8 7 6 5 4 3 2 1

Preface

This book presents a successful system of ideas and techniques that will help you discover your inner wisdom and strengths while enhancing your physical, mental, and spiritual well-being. All that is necessary on your part is to use time-tested, simple, common-sense techniques that allow you to gradually make positive changes in your life and develop your inner abilities. The term spiritual well being, as used in this book, does not imply adherence to some religion, because spirituality is not necessarily tagged with any particular form of religion. One can be spiritual in thought and action, and yet not be in accord with the fundamentals of the popular or accepted religion of the day — or with any religion, for that matter. Spirituality stems from an inborn sense of righteousness stimulated and nourished by reason and conscience.

Every human being naturally wants to have control over his or her life and to live an enjoyable and happy life. However, all desires for joy and happiness must begin with the personal aspirations of the individual.

The first time an individual cries out: "Let there be health, harmony, healing, love, kindliness, and happiness, but let it begin with me, for I will be the dispenser of these into my environment, into my world," the seeds of health and well-being, happiness and harmony, brotherhood and sisterly love, are beginning to take root. This is the point at which Peace Profound begins to unfold in the life of that individual. We are all the architects of our own fortunes and misfortunes.

In short, the essence of this book is captured in two of the Golden Verses on Practical Life Rules, attributed to that great Greek philosopher Pythagoras:

Think, before you act, that nothing stupid results; to act inconsiderately is part of a fool.

Do nothing beyond what you know, yet learn what you may need; thus shall your life grow happy.

Above all, you will learn that if you focus on your family, your friends, the needs of others, yourself, your work, and doing your very best, happiness will find you.

Robert O. Owolabi

Dedication

This book is dedicated to the memory of the victims of the September 11, 2001 terrorists attacks at the World Trade Center, New York, the Pentagon, Washington, DC, and in western Pennsylvania.

It is also dedicated to

my loving sister:

Mojisola Adenike Adelola, nee Owolabi

who died tragically

on

Monday, January 17, 2000

at the very young age of 35 years.

May the souls of the departed rest in peace. Amen

Contents

Preface iii

Introduction viii

Chapter 1. Take Care of Your Health 1

Chapter 2. Be Flexible 6

Chapter 3. Be Positive and
           Follow Your Mind 12

Chapter 4.. Deal with Problems
           as They Arise 18

Chapter 5. Avoid Anger 25

Chapter 6. Observe Moments of Silence
           (Alone!) 30

Chapter 7. Talk Less, Listen More,
           Learn More, Love More 46

Chapter 8. Achieve Happiness
           and Retain It 54

Chapter 9. Schedule Time for Fun 60

Chapter 10. Be a Volunteer 67

Contents

Chapter 11.	Pay More Attention to Your Family	72
Chapter 12.	Adopt a Code of Conduct	76
Chapter 13.	Take Time to Relax and Commune with Nature	88
Chapter 14.	Epilogue	93
	Other Books by Author	101
	Order Forms	109

Introduction

With practice and sincerity of purpose, any one can harness virtually unlimited powers of insight, creativity, and spirituality in order to achieve a life of fulfillment and happiness. One can attract good people and events in one's life. One can speed the body's natural healing processes and create harmony in one's surroundings. These abilities are universal. All one has to do is learn how to draw upon the higher knowledge already within the inner self.

Introduction

From the beginning of creation, human beings have been surrounded with problems. Social scientists and anthropologists recognize that problem solving is an essential aspect of our lives.

We human beings are faced with two kinds of problems: theoretical and practical. Theoretical problems stem from our quest for knowledge of our immediate environment and ourselves. Practical problems arise out of our perpetual need to do something, to accomplish something. To begin the process of creating and maintaining this state of self-fulfillment and perpetual bliss, we must become aware of those faculties and potentialities, undeveloped and undisciplined, that lie within. We must also become conscious of those faculties of our nature that are to some degree awakened but are nevertheless abused, misused, or inappropriately applied. Such destructive behavior—in many cases unconscious on our part—produces disharmony in our life and in the lives of those around us.

If we are to fully enjoy life, to fully utilize the "instruments" given to us for this purpose, we must become aware of who we truly are—aware of our true, composite nature and of the divine spark, which lies within us. We must fully utilize the energies of our being—the inner and outer faculties—in creating the environment that we ultimately experience.

Think not that life is without design or that it is ill planned. Life is the flowering of our thoughts and actions, the very product of our minds and hands.

Introduction

Life consists of the inner and outer faculties united as one — absorbing, reflecting, and transmitting our higher spiritual energies. When thoughts of health, wellness, harmony, healing, love, and kindliness not only reside within an individual as a general attitude of mind but also find expression in his/her daily life and engender in him/her a sense of respect for the common humanity of all people, they join with similar thoughts in the minds of millions of other people, thus forming the basis of harmony and brotherhood or sisterhood within the human race.

CHAPTER 1

Take Care of Your Health

A healthy body lends much to the enjoyment and fulfillment of life. Although it is not absolutely essential to mental and spiritual health, being physically healthy is conducive to the overall appreciation of life.

Not many adults are completely free of ailments — of one kind or another. Altogether, people spend countless billions of dollars on health measures, trying to rid themselves of pain from injury or illness.

For many ailments, there seems to be no permanent cure. Sickness always seems to be with us. No sooner is one illness cured than another arises. People are constantly searching for cures, or for aids to health. For the most part, their search is undertaken in hindsight; they wait until illness has struck before they decide to seek help. Many people do not bother to take preventive measures to bring about good health in the first place—much less to maintain it once they have it.

One could ask, What is the most important ingredient in keeping healthy? Is it diet, exercise, positive thinking, proper breathing, or something else? Good health stems from the proper practice of all of these measures. Moreover, when practiced in moderation, each of them will contribute to the overall health of the individual.

The ideal diet is a balanced one insofar as the distribution of protein, carbohydrates, fats, and other nutrients is concerned. What is more important, however, is the amount of food ingested and the frequency with which a person eats. Whether one is on a diet of rice, a diet of vegetables, or a diet of fruit, meat, and vegetables, one endangers one's state of health to a greater degree by overeating or undereating than by the choice of what one eats. Overeating, of course, taxes the digestive system and tends to bring about obesity.

Take Care Of Your Health

Undereating makes the body more susceptible to disease. Consuming a moderate but proper amount of food is probably the most important element in the general welfare of the physical system.

Exercise is perhaps second in importance, since it provides the means of maintaining proper distribution of the food ingested and the wastes excreted by the body. Without exercise, the movement of nutrients through the body is slowed, and wastes accumulate and multiply. Exercise, too, should be practiced in moderation, without an attempt to develop strength that has no purpose other than the ability to lift heavy weights. (Strength that is developed in order to satisfy a legitimate need, such as doing one's work or engaging in wholesome hobbies, is another matter.) For the average person, exercise such as walking or running is sufficient to maintain good circulation and elimination. Moderate exercise, undertaken in conjunction with moderate eating habits, is a primary requirement for good health.

The third physical asset to good health is proper breathing. While food provides the body with the necessary fuel and sustenance, and exercise permits the ingested nutrients to be properly distributed throughout the body, breathing provides the magical essence by which food revitalizes and rebuilds bodily tissue. It supplies the vital life force, the energy that maintains the body as a living entity. Improper breathing renders this process less efficient. Shallow breathing allows stale air to collect in the lung cavities, thus diminishing the good effect that air can have on health while at the same time acting as a poison or inhibitor to body processes. Regular periods of deep breathing and full exhalation serve to flush the lungs of impure or devitalized air. From a purely physical point of view, this should be done several times each day. Special breathing exercises are also tremendous aids to health. They enable us to direct the vital life force dwelling within us to certain key areas of the body with each breath we take, thereby helping the body to fight disease, sharpen consciousness, and facilitate the development of vital organs.

One factor conducive to good health that is less easy to describe—and yet is an important aspect of it—is proper thinking, also known as positive thinking. According to mystics and philosophers, the mind and the consciousness of a human being are not isolated in any given part of the body but are diffused and present in every cell of our being. Therefore, our thoughts directly affect the more subtle vibratory nature of our body parts and tissues. If a person harbors thoughts of vengeance, self-pity, fear, or envy, the vibratory nature of his/her body parts will respond to these thought-wave patterns and will be affected negatively by them. Conversely, if a person holds thoughts of love, tolerance, responsibility, kindness, and sympathy, then the vibratory nature of the body parts will respond to these thought-wave patterns and will be affected positively by them. Only in fairly recent times have mainstream therapeutic practitioners emphasized the potential effects of psychosomatic factors in the genesis of illness, yet they play a very definite role in the condition of our health. On one hand, this is the easiest factor to control, in the sense that one has only to change one's thought patterns; on the other hand, people tend to stubbornly resist making this type of change.

Here, our main concern has focused on adopting the measures outlined above for the purpose of maintaining good health. In many instances, these measures also serve to eliminate sources of illness or discomfort in the body. It is far easier, of course, to prevent illness than to eradicate it once it takes hold. Regardless of the condition of health in which a person finds himself or herself, taking steps to choose a healthful diet, engaging in appropriate exercise, practicing good breathing techniques, and entertaining positive thoughts, are bound to have beneficial results.

CHAPTER 2

Be Flexible

It is considered a mark of wisdom to be willing and able to alter one's views. To tenaciously hold on to fixed ideas which are not subject to alteration is to live blinded to the evolutionary processes that function in the world in which we live. Life might

Be Flexible

be considered as a process of evolvement, even on the most basic level of the definition.

Growth toward maturity, whether of body or of mind, is in itself a process of evolution. Through the ages, evolution has been most pronounced in the evidence of changes in life forms and change in attitudes reflected in the thought processes of individuals — or whole peoples — who populate the world. It is quite difficult for any individual living in this world to judge the purpose and intent of such a vast process. We do not have the perspective with which to see both the process and the finished product. Throughout the extensive period of time during which humans have left behind evidence of thinking, there have nevertheless been those who have recognized that the process is one of betterment, that evolution is directed toward what has been called *progress*.

Judgment alone seems to confirm, but in the technical sense may not prove, this concept. Surely, the mature adult has attained a higher, more advanced stage of evolution than a relatively helpless infant. Growth from helplessness to a certain degree of ability to sustain oneself is evidence that evolution is taking place. As individuals, we grow in another sense as well: we apply ourselves to the analysis of our environment and our relationship to the myriad of forces that act upon us. We grow in our concepts and in our understanding. What seems right or correct to us today may contain errors, which become apparent tomorrow. Conversely, what appears to be erroneous today may prove to be right at some point in the future.

If we contribute, to some degree, to our own growth, evolvement, and betterment by changing or altering our views, then we are complying with our ability to evolve and grow. From this standpoint, we conclude that evolvement is directed toward perfection. Regardless of the terminology that may be used in regard to the evolvement of humans and the aims of humans, we are constantly forced to move away from generalizations. It is almost futile to attempt to define or pin down certain concepts relating to the human condition or human aspirations, because to do so is such a difficult process.

Perfection is a good example of a concept that is virtually impossible to define satisfactorily, because no one is perfect. No human-made thought, action, or creation is a point of perfection in itself. We move toward what we conceive to be perfection because we are aware of our own imperfections, that is, our inabilities to cope with certain situations and to answer certain questions that confront us.

It is supposed that perfection is a state in which there will exist no further questions or conditions that will be subject to alteration. We might say generally, then, that the state of perfection toward which we hope to move is a state of complete understanding, complete harmony, and a sympathetic relationship with all the powers and forces that make up the universe.

Be Flexible

Can't we realize that human beings within a given country do not change their beliefs, their attitudes, or their patterns of behavior overnight? Do individuals in a democracy suddenly take on a different form of life when candidates from one political party are voted out of office and must concede power to another party? We are always in a state of transitory thinking. When we as individuals, as countries, as organizations, or as groups of any kind set ourselves up to claim that one way of dealing with an issue is perfectly right and all other ways are totally wrong, that everything is black and white, that there is no intermediate mode of response which is acceptable, that there is no possibility of compromise, we are failing to take into consideration our own imperfections and the fact that we as individuals are in a state of transition and not in a final state of perfection.

What is needed in the universe is a better awareness of what is good, a clearer conception of modes of thought and action that are consistent with the moral order of the universe. We can judge what this moral order is, but only by living, and by observing, and by learning to reach beyond the limitations of the physical world in order to contact sources of the Infinite that can be heard and felt and experienced only through the inner self. Based upon this tempering force of the good, our judgments can become more refined, so we are less likely to be placed in a position where a final judgment, or a final answer, or an absolute *yes* or *no*, must always be our conclusion. The same principle applies to the universe as a whole. A magician may be able to perform magic, and our senses may be capable of being deluded, but our intuition will whisper the truth if we but choose to listen for it.

The force of good did not come about as a result of some gigantic type-form inadvertently being tipped over, nor did the laws by which humans live come into existence accidentally. The protein molecule, which is peculiar to living beings, is so complicated that the probability that even one single living organism could have taken shape without direction from some higher force is minuscule. Therefore, it is better for us to presume that there is law and order in the universe, and that our position is that of an onlooker — that is, that we do not fully understand this law and order but we are nevertheless able to evolve in our understanding of it. Without this viewpoint there is no purpose, no good, and no hope.

If we accept the universe as the result of experimentation by forces that happened to come together in a certain way, then our efforts are useless. If, on the other hand, we view the universe as a manifestation of the emergence of the good, and we realize that the good is an evolving force that humans can draw upon to use and have as a guide, then we can predicate our actions and our concepts upon ideals that are infinite in their extent and duration.

Be Flexible

Those who have glimpsed the realities, the mystics and advanced thinkers who have tried to guide the rest of humanity, are those who have seen a little further than we have at this point, but that same line of vision is available to us if we occasionally subordinate our physical senses and take our direction and our inspiration from a source that comes from the essence of life itself, which is evidenced in our sense of intuition. In doing so, we will become more tolerant, and we will be guided to base our decisions and our lives upon the principle that nothing that is human made and human controlled will ever be wholly good or wholly evil. The ultimate good comes from a source that is beyond what humanity is capable of fabricating.

CHAPTER 3

Be Positive and Follow Your Mind

The process of positive thinking is easier than one can imagine. All it takes is resolving to see ONLY what is good in all things. Even when things look bad to the naked eye, it is still possible to look at them positively. It's simply a case of

Be Positive And Follow Your Mind

whether the glass is half full or half empty! Remember the old saying: if life gives you a lemon, turn it into lemonade. On a more humorous note, in the words of Henry Rollins — a famous American, "When life hands you a lemon, say 'Oh yeah, I like lemons. What else ya got?'" On a more philosophical level, as espoused and put so well by Einstein, "Out of clutter, find simplicity."

The mind is the most effective asset a person possesses. However, unlike organs of the body, which can be seen either by the naked eye or by x-ray machines, the mind can only be imagined. In Shakespeare's Julius Caesar, we learn that "there is no art to find the mind's construction on the face," yet the mind's construction can have a profound impact on how the body parts function.

The mind cannot be compared to other body parts. Indeed, the mind is not one of the body parts! It is in a class of its own. One may ask, how can one know one's mind? Well, my answer is, Not by reason. The function of reason is to distinguish and define. One can comprehend the mind, but only through a faculty superior to reason, by entering into a state in which one is no longer limited in one's thinking. This state is one of perpetual ecstasy. It is the liberation of one's mind from its usual state of finite (*limited*) consciousness. When one ceases to be limited, one's mind is liberated and one's spirit becomes as free as the stars.

Every idea or thought construed by the mind becomes one's reality. Everything in nature is dual:

TAKE CONTROL OF YOUR LIFE

The good is always accompanied by the bad, and the right is always accompanied by the wrong. As human beings, we are all given the free will to think what we want to think and do what we want to do. However, as in the natural law of cause and effect (*karma*), we experience the reactions to our actions, since actions and reactions are equal and opposite — one of Isaac Newton's laws of motion. Since we have this enormous ability to shape the construction of our mind, it behooves us to shape it in the form that is most beneficial to the functioning of our body.

First Rule: Always see a ray of light, in any form of darkness. All things happen for a purpose. To drive the point home, Emerson stated, "In the depths of winter I finally learned there was in me an invincible summer."

Second Rule: Always see the best in every person you encounter. By our nature as human beings, we find it easier to see what is wrong with others, especially when they are different from us in the color of their skin, in their religion, in their ethnic background, in their national origin, and so on. It takes some effort to overcome this natural human tendency, but once we work at it, it becomes part of us and we would never imagine behaving otherwise. This is not to say that we would not occasionally encounter someone who is just strange on all counts, but those people are the exceptions. Most human beings are good and have good intentions in most everything they do. Nobody I know leaves their home every day with a conscious desire to behave badly or to bring ridicule on himself or herself.

Using our free will for the good of others entails expecting and seeing the best in every human being we en-

Be Positive And Follow Your Mind

counter—be it on the street, at home, at work, at play, at church, at the mosque, in the synagogue or temple, on the bus, train, or airplane, or elsewhere. In behaving this way, some people have truly been blessed—in some cases, even to the point of encountering "angels" by chance! Sadly, others have missed out on valuable opportunities by refraining from seeing the good in others. Thus expecting and seeing the good in everyone not only enhances feelings of self-worth in the people whom one encounters, it can also be beneficial to the one who dares to view people in this way!

The positive charges emitted by people when they feel good are naturally contagious! When you do or say something nice to a person, make a point of noticing their countenance toward you. You will feel good toward them because of the positive charge they have just emitted (unconsciously) towards you. Conversely, if you are nasty to a person, through what you did or said, or even just through the way you looked at them, there is a very high probability that you will get a nasty look in return—or at least a very negative charge (also unconsciously) from them. This negative charge or nasty look will give you an uncomfortable feeling.

Now consider how it would feel to get many of those negative charges in one day! This is not good for one's psyche. In the words of Bill Lemey—a famous American, "When nobody around you seems to measure up, it's time to check your yardstick." Also, an unknown sage once said, "Better to light a candle than to curse the darkness." Last but not least on this subject, Malcolm S. Forbes once said, "People who matter are most aware that everyone else does."

TAKE CONTROL OF YOUR LIFE

Third Rule: Always give compliments. Giving compliments is the cheapest and simplest gift one human being can give to another. Even a simple smile when we encounter someone else is a form of compliment! Remember the old saying, Life is like a mirror; smile at it and it is charming; frown at it and it becomes sinister.

I have never seen many people who frown back at a smiling face! Even when people are angry at something else and they encounter somebody who is smiling, the natural tendency is to smile in return. Of course, because of the reason for their anger, the smile may be superficial or it may not last more than a split second, but more than likely they would smile at least briefly before snapping back to the current reality of their life. In the meantime, you have received a smiling face, which has psychologically made you feel warm inside.

Endeavoring to see the good in others engenders acknowledging that good with a compliment. Compliments can be given for both good and bad performances. We need to remember that nobody sets out to give a terrible performance. It usually happens when Murphy's Law kicks in: what *can* go wrong *will* go wrong. Therefore, a compliment for the effort put into a performance is in order. It makes the recipient of the compliment feel good and, in turn, gives the giver of the compliment some warm feelings inside to boot.

In the words of Nikki Giovanni—an American of Italian descent, "Mistakes are a fact of life. It is the response to error that counts." Bottom line: Always strive to say positive things to others, keeping the negative ones to yourself.

Be Positive And Follow Your Mind

You will be amazed at how much attraction and trust you will get from others if all they hear from you is good news! People will feel comfortable around you in good and bad times—perhaps even more so in the bad times, when they need someone to pick them up (figuratively, that is).

CHAPTER 4

Deal with Problems As They Arise

Problems arise in our lives more frequently than we can imagine or want to admit. In fact, problems can be regarded as necessities of life because, just like variety, problems add some *spice* to life. A life without problems would be as boring as sitting in a doctor's waiting room! In short, a person without problems is a dead person. It is how individuals deal with

Deal With Problems As They Arise

problems that makes the difference between mastering them and being broken by them.

A major part of dealing with problems is decision-making. Making decisions may be one of our most important activities, from the cradle to the grave. Decision-making skills are important to planning and living constructive, satisfying lives. We make decisions from our first waking moment each day: we decide whether to eat a big breakfast, or have some juice or coffee, or just skip breakfast altogether for that day. We decide on which clothing to wear for the day if we are not in an occupation that requires the wearing of uniforms.

We are conscious and systematic in making some choices, while others we make with little conscious effort. A sensible process or strategy of decision making, if put into practice, can yield solutions that are more satisfying. The thought and action required in making a decision demand that a person put forth time and energy. Thus the solution requires that a commitment be made. One selects a course of action and pledges to follow through with the necessary time and effort.

Each of us, because of our nature as human beings, is unique, so each decision we make is unique to some extent, at least in terms of its consequences. Different individuals may face seemingly similar situations and yet have different outcomes. Sometimes a decision may produce unwanted results — a.k.a. unintended consequences. This may be because we have direct control over the decision but not over the outcome. A well-considered decision, however, increases the probability of achieving the desired outcome. Control in our life begins with planning, choosing, and then acting with commitment. Indecision as a character trait indicates lack of confidence as well as avoidance of making commitments. It may mean trying to remain "on the fence." Indecision prevents one from moving toward one's goals, and can hinder one from attaining freedom or control over one's life.

In ancient times, people were ruled by decrees and/or rigid laws, or by specific stipulations on what was allowable according to societal norms. Nowadays, people have more freedom, and they are presented with a myriad of choices, options, and opportunities. As our society evolves, we are required to make more choices, and to do so on a more frequent basis. These increased options thrust us into new sets of conditions that impact on our personal, educational, and vocational futures. As these situations confront us, we must rise to the occasion and be decisive. Regardless of the degree of awareness of our freedom to choose, however, we do not necessarily have the know-how and self-confidence that lead to making good choices.

Indecision can lead to frustration and anxiety. Time and energy can be needlessly expended when we know that we must make a choice and yet we cannot bring ourselves to act upon the situation at hand. We may not feel confident enough to act, or we may come up with elaborate reasons why we should not act. Thus we continue to use up energy

Deal With Problems As They Arise

by procrastinating, and we continue to avoid taking action.

To overcome this type of situation, a person needs to develop a positive plan of action or strategy. Identification and adoption of new life plans will reveal the need to change undesirable characteristics or conditions. Attaining what one wants is based on the development and application of skills that help overcome obstacles. Once one has taken action to conquer indecision, confidence in one's own abilities will grow.

It is helpful to write down the pros and cons of major decisions. Important issues such as career planning, marriage, divorce, health maintenance, or retirement may present us with the need to make difficult choices. To make good decisions, we need to reflect on what is important in our life. In writing down possible solutions to problems, along with alternatives to those solutions, we can list experiences that have provided us with knowledge of our abilities, attitudes, aptitudes, and interests.

There are practical steps that one could utilize in solving almost any problem. Different people make decisions in different ways, but many of the steps involved are similar. Robert Heinlein—a famous American once said, "When faced with a problem you do not understand, do any part of it you do understand, then look at it again." The following steps are designed to help a person arrive at a decision in a logical, systematic way:

1. Identify the problem.

2. List what is already known about the problem. Do research to obtain additional information if necessary.
3. Consider possible solutions, listing the pros and cons of each one.
4. Think through the possible outcomes of the proposed solutions.
5. Make a choice, no matter how difficult it may be to do so.
6. Make a commitment to yourself in writing, and follow through on your decision.

If you have difficulty dealing with specific problems that arise in going through the process outlined above, perhaps it is because you are confused about what it is you really want out of life. Can you list three major things you really want? Are they important now? Will they influence your future plans?

If you have not achieved your goal(s) in life, identify the obstacles that are blocking you. What are the external blocks? Perhaps more importantly, what are the internal blocks holding you back? If you stay focused on *external* factors that seem to limit you, this may prevent you from seeing the *internal* limiting factors, which could very well be major contributors to your lack of success. For example, you might ask yourself, what is it that I fear might happen if I am successful in achieving a particular goal?

Now go back and repeat the six steps. Use this logical process to unlock your intuitive flow. With practice, the technique will become second nature,

Deal With Problems As They Arise

and you will find yourself making decisions almost effortlessly. The answer is in your subconscious mind. You have within you all the answers, and once you gain confidence in making decisions, you will make them almost instantaneously. Be a decider! Learn to make yourself the master of the situation, rather than allowing the situation to take control of you.

In summary, problems are inevitable in life, and we ought to know how to control and resolve them rather than letting them control and destabilize us. The following list sets out important facts and ideas to apply in dealing with a problem.

- Vagueness in defining a problem is often an obstacle to solving it.
- The more specific you can be in stating a problem, the closer you come to an answer. If you say that you would like to be happier, your statement is too vague to be helpful. It would be more appropriate to say, "I'm unhappy in my job because I have almost no contact with people."
- Being overeager to settle a problem may tempt you to try to solve it too quickly. On the other hand, you may not get a problem solved at all if you spend too much time procrastinating.
- It helps to break the problem into a series of steps. Once you have done so, think of your next step. Instead of attempting to reach the final solution all at once, take ac-

tion on one small segment. Remember that a journey of a thousand miles begins with the first step.
- Indecision adds little to—and detracts from—the attainment of joyous, autonomous living.
- The ability to make choices, decisions, and life plans is one of a person's most distinctly human attributes.
- We have in our subconscious mind (within us) all the answers. We need only to find the key to the storehouse.

CHAPTER 5

Avoid Anger

Anger is a natural state of mind that at times is either necessary or unavoidable, so it is okay to be angry when the situation warrants. Some circumstances seem to lend themselves only to anger, and if one does not become angry, one may even appear "strange" to other people (because anger is expected!).

All of us have been angry at one time or another, but only when one becomes irritated easily does anger need to be tamed. When one gets to that state of existence, one actually invites anger to take root in one's mind without realizing it. As a loving host, one invites anger to enter one's premises. The problem is that, before one knows it, this fiery rage becomes completely overpowering, and one is at a total loss as to how to subdue it.

Just what is anger anyhow, and how does it affect a person?

Anger, according to the *New World Dictionary of the American Language, Second College edition*, is "a feeling of displeasure resulting from injury, mistreatment, opposition, etc., and usually showing itself in a desire to fight back at the supposed cause of this feeling." It also went further to state that "anger is broadly applicable to feelings of resentful or revengeful displeasure." Anger affects a person in numerous ways. It destroys peace, neutralizes love, engenders hatred, and turns friends into enemies. Its outcome is to stir up strife, cause confusion, and scatter the mind. It tears down, destroys, weakens, and annihilates the finer qualities of mind and soul. It burns up all that is noble. It is a consuming blaze, born of the fires of destruction. Ultimately, all that remains of its host is a wreck of his/her better self, like a forest that has been swept by a great fire—burned out, blackened, and dead.

Such is anger, that destroying, consuming passion. Its ultimate consequence is to crush the indi-

Avoid Anger

vidual who indulges in it. Its destructive action is aimed at others, but its most devastating effect is unleashed on the person who gratifies it. It creates in that person a state of negative karma and binds her/him more securely to the fatal wheel of death and rebirth.

In fact, we must realize that anger is a very useful servant of negative power. So long as anger dominates a person's mind, it is nearly impossible for that individual to make any headway on a rational path. It is also extremely difficult for a person to concentrate on anything else as long as he/she gives in to fits of anger. The two are inimical to each other—being angry, on one hand, and concentrating, or staying focused, on the other.

In its effects, anger is more deadly to the mind than cancer is to the body. It is an ailment which afflicts its victim for the duration of his/her life. By the time physical death comes, the mind is so poisoned that there is no moral value left in it. (In addition, it must not be forgotten that this mental disease is also a factor in producing many of the common physical aliments.) This silent killer eats its way into and through the innermost moral fiber of its victim. In this sense, perhaps the great pity is that anger does not kill a person outright.

One unfortunate feature of this ugly disease is the fact that many of its sufferers are unwilling to concede that they suffer from it. They tend to insist that it is others who have it, and that they themselves are the innocent victims of the malevolence of others. To even suggest that a person is afflicted with this ailment is often sufficient to throw him/her into a violent spasm.

Another most pathetic feature of this terrible sickness is that it is one disorder that no doctor can correct. Furthermore, death does not bring it to an end. Even in future incarnations—for those who believe there is such a thing—the condition continues to ravage its victims, until they learn, through suffering and self-control, to cure themselves of the ailment. The same fate also awaits those who do not believe in reincarnation, because reincarnation is a cosmic reality that no one has control over.

Now that all the facts have been laid before us, let us make a constant effort to shun anger. And before we become sufferers of this terrible torment, let us become aware of the outward manifestations of anger: slander, evil gossip, backbiting, faultfinding, irritability, grouchiness, jealousy, impatience, resentment, destructive criticism, and so forth.

In summary, anger is a natural state of mind that is either necessary or unavoidable. However, it becomes a problem when one gets irritated easily. Then, it becomes a deadly habit that should be avoided as much as possible. While it is okay to be angry at times, it becomes a problem if it overtakes a person and becomes one's intuitive response to all feelings of injury, perceived mistreatment, or opposition. At this stage, it becomes a form of mental poisoning[1], which is detrimental to the overall well being of an indi-

Avoid Anger

vidual. Anger destroys peace, neutralizes love, engenders hatred, and turns friends into foes. It eats its way into and through the innermost recesses of its victim. And, worst of all, it does not lend itself to correction through medication. Therefore, anger, is a deadly habit that ought to be avoided at all costs.

---

[1] *Mental poisoning is a metaphysical term used to describe an invisible, often undetectable source of emotional torment, ill health, and even death.*

CHAPTER 6

Observe Moments Of Silence (Alone!)

Silence appears to be a condition that many people seem to want as little to do with as possible. The absence of meaningless babble and assorted noises is irritating to many persons and they seek to fill the void in every possible way.

Observe Moments of Silence (Alone!)

To enjoy silence is looked upon by some as an old pastime. Peace and quiet are considered worthwhile for only brief periods of time. In fact, humanity's love of continuous noise and frantic activity has given rise in history to an entire system of punishment called "The Silent Treatment."

However, in the wise words of a famous American, Adlai Stevenson, "In quiet places, reason abounds." Likewise, Pythagoras counseled that "the basic ingredient of wisdom is to learn to meditate and unlearn to talk." Observing moments of silence is more important than we ordinarily realize. Remaining silent and focusing inward are essential to the harmonious fulfillment of many of our functions as humans

During our moments of silence, we may decide to just sit quietly and wait for that "still, small voice" to talk to us. However, we may also use these golden moments to focus on certain important things in our life through visualization, contemplation, concentration, and meditation[1]. Now, what does it mean to just sit and listen to the voice within? It means that we are willing to become oblivious to our outer surroundings for a while and simply allow our inner mind to take over. This will free us up to listen and hear the voice of reason within us talking, perhaps even providing us with one or more of the following:
- answers to questions that have been on our minds,
- illumination on some confusing messages we may have been getting,

- a clearer direction to follow on our career path or in a personal relationship or business endeavor. The opportunities are limitless!

This practice of sitting quietly and listening is useful when we are confused and have no clue as to how to go about dealing with troubling matters in our life. However, if we know exactly what we want but do not know how to get it, then we can practice the arts of visualization, contemplation, concentration, and meditation during our moments of silence.

Now, what exactly do these terms mean?

Visualization

Visualization is a mental process whereby we "paint" on the "screen" of our consciousness an image, simple or complex. A person undergoing visualization is indeed painting on the screen of his mind representations of that which he desires. In his mind's eye, he gradually sees a picture of what he desires. Once he sees the picture as completely as he can visualize it, he dismisses it entirely from his mind. This transfers the image from the objective to the subjective mind—the *subconscious*—and then outwardly into space, hence literally getting it off his mind.

As a result of transmitting the positive thought into outer space, he will be drawn to those conditions and circumstances by which he can bring the visualization into reality in objective ways. The image on the screen of his mind must be so realistic as to be actualized.

Observe Moments of Silence (Alone!)

Take, for instance, somebody who currently lives in an apartment or a rented property and has a desire to purchase his own home. The process of visualization entails sitting in a quiet place, preferably with the eyes closed to avoid external distraction, and then building the type of home he wants (in his mind's eye). He will not just build the exterior of the house but will imagine what the interior will look like — that is, how large the kitchen will be; how many garages, bathrooms, and bedrooms there will be; what special features will be included in the master bedroom (for example, a Jacuzzi, a bidet, large closets, a sitting room); and so forth. In short, all the intricate details of the home will be imagined.

Then the entire idea will be let go — that is, released into space, gotten off one's mind. This is the tricky part, but it is crucial. (As an analogy, imagine dropping a letter into a mailbox. One does not go back and retrieve the letter and look at it again. If one does that, the letter will never be processed by the mail carriers and will never reach its destination.) One must let go after visualizing the image one wants, and then leave the rest to Divine Providence to do its part — that is, to make of the visualized image a reality.

Contemplation

Contemplation refers to a state of inner consciousness where one is mentally sifting — turning over in the mind's eye certain ideas or information. One does this contemplative action in order to gain various perspectives on raw data, to hopefully achieve an insight into conditions put before the mind that may be puzzling or tantalizing to the subjective sense. The subjective sense is that arena of the mind that lies just below the objective five-sense category of seeing, smelling, tasting, hearing, and touching. When one contemplates, one concentrates as best one can upon information. It is a relatively active use of the inner consciousness.

In other words, contemplation is a very subjective process, which takes place entirely within the reasoning mind itself and is independent of the external sense organs. It is the inner relation of thought — that is, instead of thinking out loud, to think inwardly and quietly. Processes that are even more subjective occur when we are visualizing and meditating. The real art of concentration leads one to turn objective thoughts inward until, through contemplation and meditation, they become ideas of the inner self.

Concentration

Concentration is the process of bringing together and the directing of our thoughts to a common center. It is the gathering, the collecting of our mental energy into a single pinpoint of undiluted, intense force. For instance, when producing maple syrup, one concentrates the sap by boiling it. Milk that is to be vacuum-packed in a can must be condensed by removing the water from it. By the same token, when we are concentrating, we are rendering our wander-

Observe Moments of Silence (Alone!)

ing thoughts less diluted by willfully rejecting the extraneous. In fact, the word concentrate means something that is undiluted, condensed, and therefore has increased strength. Our concentrated thoughts automatically become a strong force, a potent power for good.

Now let us think of concentration in the psychological, or mental, sense. We say that we are concentrating on something. Again, let us ask ourselves, Exactly what do we mean by this? It is important to expend some effort in thinking about this, because a limited understanding of the concept of concentration and its functions will limit the benefits we reap from engaging in the process itself.

To get a good grasp of the meaning of "concentrating on something," we use the following example: Suppose we want to work with something that is either minute in size or rather intricate. The task may involve threading a fine needle or inserting a very small screw into an aperture of some mechanism. We have all had experiences similar to these, and we realize that in such circumstances we cannot permit our vision to wander. Achieving the desired result requires an intense focusing of our vision on the minute objects with which we are working.

There is another way of describing this mental aspect of concentration. It is the focusing of attention. In the above example, this consisted mainly of making our faculty of concentration responsive to our *visual* impressions. In other settings, our primary focus may involve a different sense, such as *hearing* (for example, when we listen to a celebrated violinist, we focus our auditory nerves on the sound waves coming to us).

This process of making our consciousness responsive primarily to only one kind of impression introduces a very important factor in connection with concentration, namely, the relative suppression of our other senses. We temporarily subordinate the other senses to the primary sense faculty that we are using. This brings us to the relationship of consciousness to our five peripheral, external sense faculties: sight, hearing, taste, smell, and touch.

In concentrating on something, how do we command one sense to be more responsive than the others? First, it is important for us to realize that our intense concentration can alternate its focus from one stimulus, one set of impressions, to another, and that this can take place so rapidly that we are not even aware of it. (This alternation of focus, however, is not to be confused with inattention or wandering of consciousness.) For instance, when we view a movie, our consciousness shifts rapidly from visual impressions to those of sound. It may appear to us that two types of impressions are received concurrently, but under such conditions there is actually a rapid alternation of consciousness between one set of impressions and the other.

The *will* plays a fundamental role in the power of concentration. The idea, the motive or purpose, is that which arouses the will. If we *will* to do something, it is because we have the desire to do it (or, at the very least, that we wish to avoid the consequences

Observe Moments
of Silence (Alone!)

of *not* doing it!). Not all our desires are equally pleasurable from the point of view of physical satisfaction. For example, we may have an unpleasant chore to perform. On one hand, we would prefer to disregard it; on the other hand, there is the urge of *conscience*, reminding us that the chore is a duty or an obligation to be fulfilled.

The will to act attends to the prevailing, *most intense* desire at the time. In the example of the chore that we would rather not do: If the moral or ethical impulse of conscience is the stronger influence, that is the response on which our consciousness becomes focused, and we will carry out our duty in spite of our aversion to the task at hand. A weak or vacillating will implies the absence of a dominant desire. A weak will is ineffective in channeling the consciousness, that is, *focusing* it in concentration. Even though the will responds to the dominant desire, the lesser desires sometimes challenge the strength of the will. We are all aware at times of being pulled this way and that by conflicting mental motivations. The zeal, the *dynamic force* of will to direct consciousness, must be kept as free as possible from distractions, whether they are caused by external stimuli or by internal, fleeting ideas.

Suppose you want to arrive at a personal meaning of the word "knowledge," and you want it to be your own conclusion, not a definition straight out of a dictionary. You begin by thinking only of the word "knowledge." Try this with your *eyes open*. As you stare ahead, objects you see about you will be distracting, and your attention will wander to them. This indicates that the will is not yet intense enough for your intended purpose. Simply put, the word "knowledge" is not yet capable of being a compelling idea in your consciousness.

In such an exercise, one must mentally say the word "knowledge" (or any other word or idea that has been selected) over and over again until it becomes a more impressive image in consciousness than anything else perceived in the immediate surroundings.

Meditation

Meditation is basically a transformation of consciousness. What does this mean? When we meditate, we change our state of receptivity, much like tuning a radio to a different frequency, thereby rendering it more likely to receive a different station. As already explained, concentration is the focusing of consciousness. Contemplation is the inner relation of thought. In meditation, we employ concentration and contemplation, but we are more sensitive to our inner impressions than to our external senses. In other words, through concentration we turn objective thoughts inward until, through contemplation and meditation, they become the ideas of the inner self.

The purpose of meditation is total immersion in the True Being in order to bring about greater harmony and understanding, thus giving us that inner peace that can result only in true joy and happiness. When we meditate, all anxiety ceases to exist, for the physical self

Observe Moments
of Silence (Alone!)

is suspended, and with it any tension that may have been present in our mind and body.

Meditation is for us human beings what sunlight and water are for plants—their principal source of life. For human beings, meditation is also the plateau of rest before the rugged cliff of life. By meditating, we learn to observe and comprehend the beauty of life and the opportunity that is given to us to conquer or at least, temporarily ignore our imperfections. In the silence and rest of reflection, we learn to hear and feel. Upon forgetting what we apparently are, and by placing aside our views of the physical world, we merge with the true Unity. Whoever meditates, loves; for when we meditate, we dissipate the shadows of doubt and distrust, and our horizon and comprehension expand so that we learn to love.

Meditating enables us to feel more deeply and to become conscious of life in all its manifestations, although we may not be able to express it in words. Through meditation, all selfishness disappears; the I AM disappears, and the WE ARE flows through. That is why our joy and our sadness are equivalent to a greater or smaller degree of meditation. In other words, the balance between joy and sadness is, to some extent, a measure (or sometimes a direct result) of the degree to which we meditate. When we meditate, all concepts become clearer, all aberrations become dissolved, and it is possible to comprehend and find the channel that carries us to the true communion with the Cosmic, which is the true source of all happiness. Meditation permits us to comprehend our own mental states and our fears, measure our ambitions, and handle our own problems. Only

TAKE CONTROL OF YOUR LIFE

in strengthening ourselves by meditation can we live a tranquil life.

Life is beautiful, but in order to be enjoyed plentifully it must be understood, and to understand it we must seek knowledge of it profoundly. We should meditate and involve ourselves in many life activities; otherwise we would be mere robots in movement, but without true meaning or joy. By dusting the cobwebs of doubt and fear from our minds, we will see life in its entire splendor and magnificence, in its incomparable, multiple manifestations. This understanding means completely forgetting ourselves in order to resonate with our surroundings, to feel one with all. We can reach this state only through meditation and profound reflection.

Life is activity and rhythm. This is borne out by observing nature in its diverse manifestations. Let us take, as an example, a small seed that is blown by the wind. No one plants it, yet it makes contact with the earth, which in turn embraces it. It receives energy from the sun, and water from the rain, and then a small plant springs forth, which develops until it has grown into a leafy tree. The tree itself produces many seeds, which serve as food for birds. Other seeds follow the same course as the original one, and keep on multiplying without interrupting the rhythm, always giving.

As another example, let us consider a group of people working toward the same goals — unity and harmony. It is as if each one were a musical note. The group of notes forms a melody, and all are involved in following the same rhythm, as if they were floating on waves over a lake, expanding until they disappear somewhere off in the distance.

Observe Moments of Silence (Alone!)

Hardworking beings that love work live their ideal. The sweetness on their faces shows the hope that enlivens their labor. The softness of their expression and their words demonstrates their faith in their own efforts with a vision that extends indefinitely. In the way in which harmony flows, new vigor emerges, as well as encouragement, perspective, and even obstacles (which we face with reality), culminating in the crystallization of our hopes in all the beauty and splendor of harmony.

When will we reach this goal? We do not know, and it is not important that we know, as long as we have the firm conviction that we have taken the correct path towards the Truth that is and will be. We should be concerned only with our faith in the righteousness of our ideal, and persevere in our efforts until the veil of our ignorance is removed. This labor must be fulfilled by ourselves if we are to ascend a step in the great ladder of spiritual progress. Meditation gives us the key to unlock this reality; it frees us from multiple fears and opens the path of our own understanding.

When we enter into silence, our clear thoughts give us the key to the solutions of our problems, which are then clearly perceived, as if a new door were opened which had previously been closed in our minds, and our enthusiasm and energies grow with our perception.

Meditation helps us clear up the effects of the causes that we have previously set in motion, the consequences of which we are now feeling. It confirms the fact that we have labored, and are still laboring, to fulfill our own destiny. A serene and contemplative life enhances our creativity and understanding.

Meditation is a regular necessity for our being,

for it is the link that seals harmony. If we do not meditate regularly, we are more likely to incur errors of understanding and to commit injustices, though not necessarily deliberately. We feed and dress ourselves, we sleep, and we work, all on a regular basis, so why don't we meditate with the same regularity? The use of our common sense accompanies an awakened consciousness; we cannot make the most of our common sense if we do not meditate.

In order to meditate, it is not necessary to place ourselves in an inaccessible place, convert ourselves into hermits, or cover ourselves with special clothing. We can meditate each day in our own homes, while we do our daily chores, in the office or on the bus or train on our way to work. This is because we carry the Holy Altar in each one of us, and in it dwells the wise Master who is always ready to speak to us. All that is required is that we retreat into the inner depths of our mind and listen to His voice, with a firm purpose to share the fruits of His knowledge unselfishly.

When we cease all thought and all desire, it is possible for us to hear the inner voice of the wise Master that dwells in the temple of our hearts. When we separate ourselves from the noise, we come closer to the Truth. In this way we can achieve the Peace Profound that is attainable only through meditation.

It should be noted that each of the subject matters described above — visualization, contemplation, concentration and meditation is more thoroughly explained in other books with particular focus on the subjects. It is acknowledged that the explanations given above are not exhaustive on them in an effort not to shift the focus of

Observe Moments of Silence (Alone!)

this book away from the actual subject matter of the book. So, readers interested in more in-depth information on these four tools of inward focusing and mental processing should explore further through their local libraries.

Exercises on Concentration

For practical application of the concentration techniques just described, the following exercises can be tried.

Exercise Number One:

Think of the color *blue*. Mentally concentrate; that is, focus your attention on the color blue. *See it* in the mind, but with *your eyes open*. Use your will to dismiss distracting impressions of things around you. At first, it may help to visualize a common thing associated with the color blue. For example, see in your mind a clear *blue* sky. This should be relatively easy. Then gradually eliminate from your consciousness the image of the sky, so that the color blue alone remains.

Exercise Number Two:

Next, try the same exercise — exercise number one but with the eyes *closed*. It will be less difficult than the former one. However, you will find that fleeting thoughts from memory will tend to arise in consciousness to conflict with your will (that is, your desire) to think of *blue* alone. You may also practice mentally concentrating on ideas other than colors, perhaps a symbol such as a triangle, cross, or circle. In any case, avoid a complex idea, that is, one that is composed of several elements that may have equal attentive value.

Exercise Number Three:
Now try another exercise in concentrating on a mental image: First, think of a dot (●). See this dot clearly in your mind. Next, see two dots (●●) clearly in your mind, then three dots, then four. Finally, see in your mind a *series* of dots as in the following illustration:

● ●● ●●● ●●●●

This time, do not see the dots separately; rather, concentrate on the image of them all at one time, *the whole series*. Do not merge them but — to repeat — concentrate on the picture of the complete series of dots: the one, the two, the three, and the four.

Exercise Number Four:
For the final exercise, visualize a circle made of cord or ribbon. *Mentally* see this circle *begin* to form at the center of your back. Next, visualize it gradually moving around you until you are entirely encircled by it. Do not see only part of the circle at a time, but let your consciousness mentally see it as one line moving around until it is surrounding you. Simply, mentally watch the *extension* of the circle from its beginning to its completion. You will find this difficult at first, but through the practice of concentration combined with visualization, you will find the final results gratifying.

Observe Moments of Silence (Alone!)

There is one principal difference between *concentration* and *contemplation*, and that is the difference in the *use* of consciousness. Concentration is primarily the focusing of consciousness, or attention, on externals, that is, things outside ourselves that register on our objective senses, such as our consciousness of hearing, seeing, and so on. Contemplation is a more subjective process, which takes place entirely within the mind itself and is independent of the outside sense organs. This subjective process occurs when we are visualizing and even in meditation.

---

1. *For those who are religiously inclined, prayers could also be offered at such times. Since this book does not treat religion or religious doctrine, we refrain from any further discussion of prayer here.*

CHAPTER 7

Talk Less, Listen More, Learn More, Love More

Talk Less

"The basic ingredient of wisdom", according to Pythagoras, "is to learn to meditate and unlearn to talk." Talk less with your mouth. Listen more with your Inner Ear. Learn more with your mind.

Talk Less, Listen More,
Learn More, Love More

Love more with your heart and soul. And live life fully and abundantly as you walk along your chosen path toward a happy and fulfilling life.

This chapter covers four distinct topics—talking, listening, learning, loving—each of which could be treated in and of itself. They are so closely related in our everyday living and in our personal development, however, that the ideas put forth here can more effectively contribute to an understanding of the unfoldment and realization of the fullness of Life if the four of them are discussed as a unit.

There is profound truth in the statement that listening is frequently more important than talking. The spoken word is like an egg—once let out of its shell (the mouth) can hardly be recovered, or put back in its shell. A very reticent person grabs more attention when he/she speaks than a loquacious person. The only person one hears when one speaks is oneself. However, when one listens, one hears almost every statement uttered by others around. To hear is simply to become conscious of sound, while to listen is to make a conscious effort to hear. We may hear without listening, as in the case of words uttered in an adjoining room, or we may listen without hearing, which is likely to occur if we are listening to a distant speaker.

Listen More

In listening, the ear is intent upon the sound. In paying attention, the mind is intent upon the thought. Listening, however, implies some attention to the meaning or import of the sound. Therefore, the Art of Listening consists of both of these, but to listen intently and fully with the Inner Ear[1] is to absorb the message and as a result, draw a closer relationship to the ideals and aspirations of the Inner Self. Too often, we have a tendency to listen "when we want to" and to disregard the real purposes of listening. We may say, 'make me want to listen, I dare you.' (Then if we are distracted, we can claim that it's not our fault but the speaker's.) We have to cultivate the desire to listen in order to be a truly good listener.

    The person who resolves to listen carefully will take the first step toward being a good listener. This resolution by itself, however, is not enough. Without consciously convincing oneself that one should listen and that one wants to listen, one is not likely to become a good listener. Through the effective use of this valuable Art of Listening, combined with the development of the physical and psychic senses, we are constantly learning and evolving. We are living and hoping to acquire a better knowledge of the purpose and the course of life. Whatever we do to achieve that end is part of our learning. In the process, we cannot forget that we are human beings, with certain physical limitations and lack of knowledge, and that we need to develop and learn through experience with certain physical laws. If this were not so, we would not be here in the first place.

Learn More

    The fact that we need to learn and master certain physical laws is evidence that we should be able to gain

Talk Less, Listen More, Learn More, Love More

a certain degree of control and knowledge by studying and observing our environment. As an analogy, the disciple who asks his Master to teach him how he may cross the water by walking upon it must first analyze his need. If there is a bridge available, why should it be necessary to walk on the water?

As human beings, we live in two separate ways — public and private, and learn in two different worlds — natural and supernatural. Nature may be called the world of time and space. All that we do in the world of Nature takes time to be accomplished, and space has to be overcome. The more space, the more time it takes, in general. And when we learn through the manifestations of Nature, this, too, takes time.

The things we learn which allow us to live safely and comfortably in this world — the temporal things — are learned in time and can be forgotten in time. The Soul, on the other hand, knows nothing of time. It is in Eternity. Therefore, the things we learn which result in evolution of the Soul Personality must be learned in Eternity. To express it in another way, the things we must learn in time are not remembered, and must be relearned (in the next incarnation, and the one following it, and so on, for those who believe in reincarnation!). The things we learn in Eternity through the experiences of the Inner are eternal, and so are never forgotten. They become a permanent expression in our Soul Personality.

Now the thoughts in this chapter particularly, or in this book in general, should present you with some keys to learning. What you may remember having studied can never be a direct means of evolution. Similarly, you cannot instantaneously and intuitively learn any of the things you need to know in order to live efficiently in this world.

Love More

In an article written by anthropologist Ashley Montagu entitled "The Awesome Power of Human Love," he states that "the single most important force in shaping our physical, emotional and spiritual lives is the power of Love." Webster's dictionary defines love as a "feeling of strong personal attachment induced by sympathetic understanding, or by ties of kinship... Ardent affection... Benevolence." By combining the many facets that contribute to the Art of Loving, such as patience, tolerance, grace, and affinity, we recognize the importance of loving with the heart and mind in the creation of impersonal, unqualified Cosmic Love.

The individual who expresses and exhibits the Art of Loving finds himself loved and admired by his fellow human beings. A child raised in an unloving environment fails to learn to love, and therein lie the problems of juvenile delinquency and emotional inadequacy. The Art of Loving is an emotional and sensitive feeling of great exhilaration. The simplicity of this impersonal, Cosmic Love is realized only after many years of practicing compassion, tenderness, and affection toward others (as we are taught in our different faith traditions, for those who have one, or family tradition, for those who don't). This great power (Cosmic Love) gives us a sense of oneness, accompanied by a consciousness of security.

Divine, Cosmic Love sees no distinction among

Talk Less, Listen More, Learn More, Love More

persons. It is Principle, and it feels its own perfection everywhere. It feels the same in the heart of the lowly as in the heart of the saint. Love *is* God, and love is *of* God. When we realize this fully, we begin to love our fellow human beings. It is a Divine, Cosmic Ordinance. As we allow the Love of God to pour out of our lives in Charity, we forgive a multitude of sins, not only in ourselves but also in others. As previously mentioned, to be loved is a great joy. To love is to increase that joy a thousand-fold. To possess and emanate a feeling of true, unqualified, impersonal love is joy beyond comprehension. To manifest this joy of the Art of Loving is to add to the fullness and efficiency of living a truly worthwhile and abundant life.

The Connection

In our individual lives, it is important that, on a regular basis, we find the ways and means of living a truly worthwhile and abundant life. We must recognize the importance of first learning to understand ourselves. We must learn to use our mind to create loftier goals for ourselves and to establish a fresh sense of confidence in our way of living.

How do we do this? First and foremost, we must have a purpose for living—and this purpose must not be wholly selfish. It must of necessity include the welfare of others. Unlimited powers lie within every one of us, and an abundant supply surrounds us. In order to exert these powers, we need to awaken the Master

TAKE CONTROL OF YOUR LIFE

Within, who can manifest only through us. He is the God of our Hearts, an inseparable part of us. He acts in conformity with our thoughts, feelings, and desires. God, then, manifests through you and me, but we must provide the channel through which He can express Himself. The warehouse of the Great Cosmic Supply is all around you. You can have anything of a good and constructive nature that you desire. By properly working with the laws of the Cosmic, you can bring about the manifestation of your ideals.

On a practical level, we realize that everything in life is transitory, changing and becoming. We ourselves change from month to month and year to year. We know that these changes can be for the good if they come about through proper thinking and proper direction of effort. The Art of Living carries with it a challenge to DARE TO DO. Over time, and with diligence and persistence, we develop the courage and confidence to cope with the vicissitudes of Life.

Slowly but surely, as we practice all the laudable ideas and principles espoused in this book, we will move toward the Light. We will develop a strong faith in the Divine Intelligence, which will assure us that our desires and aspirations will be realized. We should be glad and give thanks for life and its experiences, for the privilege that is ours, thankful that we are able to solve our problems, and grateful for our moments of happiness. Put these principles into practice, and live them daily! Realize that, as a human being, you are divine by nature, and that you are entitled and expected to manifest that aspect of the divine, which lies within you. Become acquainted with your Inner Self, the Master Within.

Talk Less, Listen More, Learn More, Love More

This is the Master to whom you may turn for guidance and inspiration.

And so, my dear reader, we have come to understand the close relationship between Listening, Learning, Loving, and Living. As we listen, we learn. As we learn, we develop the quality and understanding of unqualified love, which in turn fills our lives with mystical understanding. Ultimately, we gain the ability to live a full, efficient, worthwhile, and abundant life.

Thus we see the great importance of listening. A good listener is open minded, and is open to learning. He who is open-minded is open hearted. The openhearted person practices the Art of Loving in his/her daily life. He who is open hearted is kingly. He who is kingly is godly. He who is godly is infinite. He who is infinite is immune. He who is immune is immortal.

---

1. *The Inner Ear refers to the psychic ear, not the physical inner ear.*

CHAPTER 8

Achieve Happiness And Retain It

Happiness is a mental, emotional, and infinite state of inner peace. Happiness is love, which engenders sacrifice — and, to some extent, even suffering. The degree to which a person experiences happiness at any given time depends on his state of evolution, which is a reflection of the relative importance that he places on the spiritual and material aspects of life.

Achieve Happiness And Retain It

The optimist enjoys intense happiness to a greater extent, and in a larger variety of ways, than the materialist or the atheist, let alone the pessimist. By his general nature, attitude, and outlook on life, the optimist develops a greater comprehension of life; thus he practices and experiments with the teachings and laws of nature on a grand scale, which helps to promote his internal evolution.

Here are some basic, concrete ways in which you may find more happiness in your daily life:

1. Stop and observe how the river follows its course, join with it (in spirit, at least), and ignore the passage of time.
2. Forget about your surroundings, and carefully listen to the song of a bird, admire the morning dew, observe the movements of the branches of the trees, and feel the fresh breeze upon your face.
3. Appreciate the birth of a new day, and thank God for being able to enjoy this rebirth.
4. Be aware of the joy you experience in feeling the warmth of family and friends.
5. Radiate pure friendship and love to others, always taking care not to hurt anyone, offering joy instead of sadness.
6. Get up in the morning with the realization that there is work to do, and that there are duties to fulfill and services to offer to others.
7. Sit quietly, read a good book, and learn something new.
8. Enjoy the company of people who share your

beliefs.
9. Engage in meditation, and raise grateful thoughts to God for the blessings that come your way.
10. Help others to understand the basic tenets of your religion or belief system, but without trying to impose your beliefs on them.
11. Shower others with affection, and be courteous to all, without prejudice of class, race, sex, sexual orientation, national origin, social position, religion, or education.
12. Keep in mind that spiritual evolution is reached by following the laws of God, and that the degree to which you grow in Illumination is commensurate with the extent to which you keep these laws.
13. Adapt to the environment by making good use of your intelligence together with the knowledge you have acquired.
14. Use the energy that springs from your Inner Self in order to carry out the activities or projects that bring joy and benefits to others.

Just as there are many paths to God, so there are many paths that lead to happiness. Harboring positive thoughts and maintaining an attitude of optimism toward the goals we wish to fulfill will bring us closer to getting there. We can always start by smiling, which not only enables us to feel happy but gives others a mental lift as well.

Once we have attained happiness, we naturally want to hold on to it. The following measures may help us in

Achieve Happiness And Retain It

doing so:

1. Strengthening the spiritual bonds of love with others
2. Making a concerted effort to gain an understanding of why we are happy, and sharing our insights with others
3. Having faith in a superior Being who can be accessed through the Divine Creation
4. Associating happiness with the sublime magnetism that enables us to comprehend the union of our psychic energies with our Cosmic energies
5. Observing a silent prayer that springs from the Inner Self, recognizing the greatness of the Great Architect of the Universe who abides in our hearts
6. Keeping in mind that our body is a sacred temple of God, and fulfilling our duty to take care of it
7. Affirming that the divine and vital spark which was activated at our birth is perfect and eternal, and that it reached us with our first breath, as an inheritance from the Creator of the Universe
8. Feeling and hearing the Divine Voice, our intuition, which guides us with love and charity
9. Bringing happiness to others through practice of the teachings of our religion or belief system (Judaism, Christianity, Islam, Buddhism, and so forth)
10. Serving others without expecting recognition or reward

11. Reciprocating favors received, avoiding the sin of omission
12. Recognizing happiness through humility and wisdom, joined in a fraternal purpose: to love others as we love ourselves
13. Deriving joy from participating in activities that help improve the quality of life of others
14. Maintaining an awareness of being an integral part of creation, but recognizing that there is something else, the Universal Force (Supreme Being, God, Yahweh), which governs us with its laws and gives us the opportunity to realize our dreams
15. Seeking to know and understand the enlightenment that derives from our spiritual and material progress, and generously imparting it to others
16. Developing a spirit of charity and fraternity that will enable us to enjoy life in Profound Peace
17. Savoring the feeling of joy, security, and peace that comes from acting or proceeding correctly

Happiness may rapidly disappear when jealousy, vanity, pride, resentment, or vicious criticism enters the picture — and perhaps even more so when one sets out to inflict vengeance on another. Charity, morals, and prudence are the three pillars that preserve happiness, which is the source of mental peace that maintains harmony of mind, spirit, and body — and in the process keeps illness at bay. It is through happiness that we reach the culmination of our spiritual evolution, thereby

Achieve Happiness
And Retain It

achieving an understanding of the importance of self-fulfillment and complete control over life's challenges. To be in a state of happiness is to calmly adapt to every situation in life with a positive attitude, like true optimists. If we are to seek happiness, we must know ourselves so that we may understand others. Happiness is, in summary, the harmony revealed in our body and its various parts, united and working together.

CHAPTER 9

Schedule Time for Fun

One may ask, how does one schedule time for fun? Good question! Of course, one could just as well ask, how does one schedule time for work? for chores? for a trip to the dentist? In short, one arranges time for fun in the same way one sets aside time for other activities.

Schedule Time For Fun

Fun is a relative term, because what is fun to one person may be a chore—or even a disgusting activity—to another. We are not even going to attempt to characterize what does or does not constitute fun. The purpose of this chapter is to remind us of the old adage: "All work and no play makes Jack a dull boy."

We all lead busy lives, and it appears that these days there just aren't enough hours in one day for us to accomplish as much as we would like. Compounding the problem is the emergence of the two-income household. In the past, when most women stayed home, there appeared to be more time for "fun things." Perhaps women had more time at their disposal in those days to plan fun times for the family.

To live a full, happy, and balanced life, it is important to take time to smell the proverbial roses. For a busy professional who wants to put in a command performance at work, this is a tough requirement! It is tough because it seems unwise, or even embarrassing, to tell your boss (much less your subordinates!) that you want to take time off to go and do fun things when there are deadlines to be met.

Family-related emergencies—such as sudden illness of a family member, inability to find a substitute for a vacationing babysitter, or the need to stay with an elderly parent who fell and broke a hip but lives 5,000 miles away—all sound legitimate, and almost nobody would fault a person for taking time off to attend to those matters. But take time off for fun things? Forget it!

Now, don't get me wrong. Some bosses may even encourage their subordinates to take time off to enjoy themselves. Trust me, those bosses are the exception, not the rule! So what are you to do if you have a typical boss? Well, you've got to do what you've got to do! A certain amount of fun and recreation is essential, and it augurs well for a happy, balanced life, but it's up to you to arrange times for doing fun things.

First, you have to determine what those things are. As mentioned earlier, fun is a relative term. What is good for the goose may not be good for the gander. One thing, however, is for sure: By "fun things," we are not necessarily talking about taking a vacation! Don't get me wrong. Vacations can be fun, but in many instances, especially on family vacations, it just doesn't work out that way. A vacation is likely to be more fun if it is taken alone, or with a partner, or with a group of your bosom friends, but that's it! When others are involved, sorry, there will be too many people to care for, thus reducing the amount of fun.

This chapter is actually about being a little "selfish" at times and doing those things that you really enjoy, so let's explore what some of those fun things might be. How about going out to lunch? L-u-n-c-h??? Yes, lunch! Believe me, going out to lunch can be a lot of fun if it is well planned and done right.

We human beings, no matter how awkward, rigid, disciplined, or serious-minded we may be, have our own "types" out there. After spending four hours at work—either attending boring meetings, writing difficult reports or proposals, or engaging in some brain-twisting technical analysis—what a difference a relaxing lunch break can be! This is especially true if you are in the company of friends whom you can relate to and speak your mind with, without any inhibitions. You will

Schedule Time For Fun

come back to the office refreshed, energized, and happy, and the rest of the work day will be a breeze! Try it! You'll like it!

If going out to lunch is not your thing, let me suggest two substitutes for this activity. The first is working out at a gymnasium or exercise spa. This is easiest for those who have a gym at work. Remember, most people have only one hour for lunch. If you do have a gym, you are in luck. Again, it's more fun if some of your favorite people go with you. If not, you will have to make new friends at the gym. My experience with things like this is, the more the merrier — by which I mean more of the type of people you can relate to.

The other activity you can engage in during your lunch break is shopping. This is primarily a female thing. I don't mean to be chauvinistic, but it is a fact! Women, in general, enjoy shopping more than men do. Most men go shopping only when they have something in particular that they want to buy. Women do, too, but when they get there, their "gathering instincts" often take over, so they end up tarrying longer at the shopping center or mall just to browse. On the contrary, men, who are "hunters" by nature, tend to go shopping only to hunt down what they have in mind, get it, and pay for it, and then out they go! In any case, you can go shopping for pleasure on your lunch break if that is an activity you enjoy. Remember, the idea here is to do what is fun for you. Again, find coworkers of similar persuasion and go out with them. If you do, you will come back to the office refreshed and ready to face the rest of the day with vigor and enthusiasm.

How about after-work activities? Well, one pos

sibility is a sort of after-work party, otherwise known as happy hour. Yes, going to a club or restaurant after work with some friends of like mind can be fun. After a tedious day at work, this can be quite relaxing. Once you get there, loosen your tie if you're wearing one, have a drink or two, have a hearty chat, do some visual flirting with people of the opposite sex (God will understand!), and then go home relaxed, refreshed, and happy. You will definitely get a good night's rest, and you will wake up the following morning feeling quite energized and ready to go to work. Of course, this is not something you would want to do every day! (If it is, you may have a serious problem on your hands!)

    Weekends can be tedious or boring, depending on the specifics of your situation — married (with or without children), single, male, female, retired, and so on. Again, we are talking about what you can do for fun, not just anything to occupy your time.

    Believe it or not, some people actually find pleasure in getting involved in church, mosque, synagogue, or temple activities. Yes, they do, for a variety of reasons! Some people are so religiously inclined that they would rather be in the company of other religious "types" than elsewhere. For such people, even doing work for the parish, such as making a casserole for a parish dinner with other church folks, may be more fun than, say, going to a concert.

    Hey, that is the idea! And that is why I said, earlier on, that fun is a relative term. For some, taking their kids to their basketball, baseball, or soccer game and watching them play is fun. So be it! For others, drinking beer with friends while watching a football game to

Schedule Time For Fun

gether is fun. Sounds good to me! For still others, weekends are a time when they would rather go watch a movie with their partner, members of their family, or their buddies. Hey, if this is what you like, go for it! As long as you derive pleasure and relaxation from engaging in an activity, it is fun. The bottom line is, if you feel afterwards that you have had an enjoyable time, then you have had fun.

Some people find that volunteering for their favorite charities is what gives them their kicks[1]. Believe it or not, this is a source of joy and satisfaction for some folks, and, by golly, it's a good thing that there are people like that! The gym or exercise spa is another place where some go on weekends to have fun. I know men who, in addition to working out themselves, go there to watch beautiful women in their skimpy exercise outfits. Even some women have confessed to going to exercise spas to admire muscular men, because to them, muscular men are strong — and therefore sexy! Anything that gives you fun is okay, as long as you do not infringe on the rights or freedom of others.

How about hobbies? Some derive fun from their favorite hobbies: tennis, golf, basketball, skiing, fishing, hunting, stamp collecting, coin collecting, model-train collecting, music, reading, and so on. The list is endless. Just like the activities discussed previously, you should make a point of scheduling time for your hobbies — and they should be pursued on a regular basis — if they are fun for you.

To summarize: As part of your path toward a happy and fulfilling life, you need to have fun on occasion, and you need to make a point of scheduling time for fun. Remember that there is no hard and fast rule for this. And the activities listed in this chapter are, by no means, exhaustive. There is a zillion other activities that could be fun to do as well.

What gives one person fun, joy, and satisfaction or fulfillment may turn others off. All you need to do is find your own niche activity, and then enjoy doing it! You will find that it enhances your life and gives you a greater sense of satisfaction and happiness.

---

1 *The next chapter is devoted to the topic of volunteering and being of service to others*

CHAPTER 10

Be A Volunteer

The willingness to be of volunteer service to others is a form of devotion, which pays spiritual dividends beyond all imagining. But one should not volunteer with the expectation of some reward or compensation, though one will surely be blessed by God — and perhaps honored by the community as well. One should volunteer because it feels good to help others, especially those who would otherwise not receive the type of help or service rendered. When one has been blessed in life, one owes it to one's community to "give back" in some way, and this is best done through volunteer service to others.

There are numerous opportunities to volunteer in almost any community. If a person belongs to a church, synagogue, mosque, or temple, that could be the first point of inquiry for opportunities to do volunteer work. For those who have no faith community, local institutions such as libraries, the fire department, the department of parks and recreation, and the department of social services — to mention a few — can always use volunteers. The essence of this chapter is not to list all the possibilities for volunteering, which would be an impossible task in any case, but rather to bring into focus the basic tenets and benefits of volunteering.

In addition to taking time out to participate in various forms of volunteer activities, one could practice some basic gestures that would generate an inner sense of gratification similar to that, which is achieved in formal settings of volunteer service. For instance, on a daily basis you could seek to share what you can spare, even if you can do so only in small ways or in meager amounts. You could go out of your way to find out where the services you are capable of providing, or the money or material things you can afford to give, would truly be a blessing to some needy person, possibly to many.

In performing random acts of kindness or generosity, accept no personal thanks for any nice gesture you bestow, any gift you give, or any help you render. When thanks are expressed by the recipient, make it your custom to say, "Please do not thank me, because it is I who am grateful. I sought to serve and give back to the community some of what I have been blessed with; you have

Be A Volunteer

afforded me the opportunity to do so. But now, the obligation to pass it on rests with you; may you, too, find an opportunity to serve someone else." Do not feel obligated to memorize these words verbatim. Once you get the gist of the words, you can express them in your own words. For example, you could simply say, "Don't thank me; it would be more gratifying to me if you were to do the same for others." (If the recipient becomes curious and wants to know more, feel free to share your religious beliefs, or whatever it is that motivates you to be of help.)

    Also, accept no gifts of a material nature for any volunteer service you render, unless you decide to accept it for the sole purpose of giving it to charity. At the moment of accepting such a gift, inform the giver that you will pass it on to someone in need of it, or to some organization or institution that will use it to continue to carry on its mission of relief and help. This is especially important in the case of gifts of money — or of items that directly satisfy basic human needs, such as food and clothing — since you can easily find someone who could make use of them.

    Always bear in mind that the more volunteer service you render, the more blessings you receive. This is a basic law of nature. As you seize each opportunity to give (and do so with the utmost spontaneity), so will future blessings be granted to you, whether or not you seek them. The greater the degree of spontaneity, with little or no thought as to personal sacrifice, the greater will be the spiritual compensation that comes your way.

    Whether you are able to go directly to the aid of another person — be it a neighbor, a friend, or a stranger, and regardless of race, creed, or color — to render aid in an emergency, or must resort to soliciting help from someone else, your intentions and efforts are impressive and laudable. In peace and quiet, perform your good deeds, render your volunteer service, and go back to your home with as little recognition as possible. The Divine Mind, or God, or Yahweh, or Allah, who sees you perform your good deeds in private, will reward you abundantly in public.

In summary, it is important to know that in the process of volunteering service to others, we should always remember one of the fundamental principles of the natural law[1] of compensation: For each sorrow or joy we cause others, we shall have experiences in like degree and manner and, at times, when the lessons to be gained thereby will be the most impressive. This principle does not exact an eye for an eye or a life for a life, for there is no vengeance involved in the process, and no intention to cause suffering for anyone. It only affirms Newton's third law of motion: Actions and reactions are equal and opposite.

---

1. *"Natural Law is the law or set of laws decreed in The Beginning by the Divine Mind as the working basis of all creation and without which no manifestation can occur or exist. Such laws are universal as to scope and manner or operation. Natural law operates on all planes and in all kingdoms alike. Natural laws are extremely simple and direct, as all such fundamental laws must be. Their mission is to ensure progressive gradations or cycles of evolution in spite of all obstacles placed by humans to thwart their operation. Therefore, natural laws establish such powers, functions, attributes, and phases in the various kingdoms of the universe as will unswervingly impose strict adherence to these laws in the pursuit of the ideal in each plane, kingdom, class, etc. The idea, the motive, behind natural laws is the preservation of life for the attainment of the ideal expression. As such, they recognize no*

Be A Volunteer

man-made ideal, no man-made law, no dictates of civilization where these are contrary to the best purposes as decreed by the Divine Mind. Natural law is always constructive — even when it seems indisputably destructive. In this it follows the method symbolized by the "Law of the Triangle." Natural law is that basic principle which, while demanding, commanding, and insisting on strict obedience to its dictates throughout, is elastic enough in one sense to allow for much and frequent blending of the entities of any plane as long as such blending harmonizes with its purposes."

CHAPTER 11

Pay More Attention to Your Family

As human beings, we are endowed with the ability to make choices about many aspects of our lives. We can choose our spouses, friends, coworkers, business associates, acquaintances, and so on. The list is endless. But one thing we cannot choose is our family. We are born into it and become stuck with it! Over time,

Pay More Attention To Your Family

we get accustomed to our family members, regardless of how we feel about them. However, while friends may desert us, spouses may divorce us, acquaintances may keep their distance (even permanently), and coworkers may go their different ways once the employment we share with them terminates, one's family will always be one's family, no matter what, and will always be there for us. It is important to safeguard and nourish this perpetual source of love and support in our lives.

In contemporary times, our family is not just a group of wonderful folks related to us by blood or marriage, but consists of all those people with whom we share intimacy. We mirror to each of them and they to us, what the world is and who we are. Thus our experience of family can either be uplifting or utterly devastating—there is no guarantee that the ways of thinking and behaving taught to us by our family will work in this world. The good news is that in this day and age, we have choices, because we have entered into a wonderful new age in which strict definitions of family are no longer the norm, thus allowing us to share more fully with those who nurture our spirit.

Some pessimists cry that the family is dying as an institution and faces certain extinction. Well, this is true only in the sense that the old rules and definitions no longer automatically apply. Emerging gradually is a new, more dynamic family structure, which will become a greenhouse for spiritual development. It is like the difference between a geodesic dome and a traditional frame house. The traditional house needs well-defined interior walls to hold up the roof and support the outside walls. The geodesic dome, on the other hand, needs no interior walls, because the interconnected triangles that make up the exterior structure support each other. Inside the dome, walls are needed only to the extent to which they satisfy the desires of the inhabitants. For our well being and peaceful coexistence, we owe it to ourselves and to our families to help create unique, wholesome ways to adapt to this new environment, and make the best of it to our utmost advantage.

    Changes in people's thinking about family are everywhere these days, as evidenced in the many volumes on healing our inner child, healing the dysfunctional family, and so forth. The golden idols of success, wealth, and fame are losing their importance. We have finally begun to realize our need to nurture and be nurtured. A quiet revolution is happening all around us in which women and men are inventing new ways to work, serve, and play—ways that allow them to share more of their time (quality time!) with their loved ones. We have begun to live in the NOW, rather than waiting until AFTER the next report, project or promotion.

    There is a dawning recognition in this very busy time that we need to nurture each other continuously, not just on an occasional weekend or evening. We are even discovering that there are things families can do together besides watching TV. Fortunately, many companies and organizations are beginning to recognize the benefits to be gained from spending time with our families, and are facilitating flexible and creative new ways to meet this need.

    Even in the best of circumstances, balancing the needs of self, children, parents, close friends, work, professional organizations, and social institutions can be an

Pay More Attention To Your Family

enormous juggling act. It seems so much easier to take the path of least resistance and avoid some of this contact, yet with the entire struggle and strain comes additional mastery of some facet of our lives. And when we least expect it, we are graced with moments of pure magic.

Envision driving home after a hectic, frustrating day at work and hearing a two-year-old in the back seat ask, "Where do the stars come from, Mommy?" or "Can I sit on your lap when we get home, Daddy?" And think of how good you feel when a friend telephones to say, "You know, that idea you gave me really worked. You are always so positive. You always help me to see the positive side of what's happening." Can there be any doubt about the need to share our special view of the world with someone who is receptive to it?

So, my dear reader, family plays an important role in promoting a balanced, fulfilling, and happy life. Whether or not you have children of your own, you have a responsibility to your family to nurture each person's spirit. You need to begin right here and now, by reaching out to someone. Endeavor to spend time with someone today. Perhaps there is someone in your family who needs nurturing. Perhaps there is an acquaintance that needs a helping hand or a sympathetic ear. It is only a conversation away.

Remember that in the process of learning to take complete control of your life, you are also learning to see with your heart and to feel that you are a part of all that surrounds you. Your greatest successes don't always entail winning the race. Furthermore, in this great and laudable endeavor, you will never be alone. The love of your family will always surround you.

CHAPTER 12

Adopt a Code Of Conduct

Perhaps only in some of the old monasteries of India, or those in Tibet, could one live strictly in accordance with all the ancient regulations, but those presented here can be adopted by most people. From practical experience, it is reasonable to state that

Adopt A Code Of Conduct

most of these can be adhered to by any man or woman without interfering with the necessary duties and obligations of present-day living. It is also reasonably likely that most people with very strong self-discipline and self-control are already living their lives in accordance with the rules suggested here, thereby contributing significantly to their own advancement, to the joy of their associates in family and business, and to the betterment of humanity generally. It will profit you greatly to try adopting as many of these rules as possible.

1. Upon arising in the morning, start the day with a prayer of thankfulness to God for the return of consciousness, because of the opportunities it affords you to continue the Great Work and mission of your life. Facing east, take seven consecutive deep breaths of fresh air, exhaling slowly after each one, and concentrate on the vitality going to each part of your body to awaken the psychic centers. Then bathe, and drink a glass of cold water before eating.

2. Upon retiring at night, give thanks to God for the day and its fruits. Ask the Cosmic Hosts to accept your psychic services while you sleep, to use your consciousness as they desire, and —

if it should please God — to grant you another day of life on Earth. Then, with thoughts of love for all living beings and a sense of peace and harmony with the entire universe, close your eyes and fall asleep, visualizing your inner self in the consciousness of God. That is, imagine that, while you sleep, your spirit would be in harmony with the spirit of God.

3. Before each meal, wash your hands thoroughly and hold them, palms downward, over the plate of food for a fraction of a minute. Then mentally pray that God will bless the food you eat, and that it will be magnetized with the spiritual radiation from your hands so that it supplies the needs of your body. Before eating the first morsel, say mentally: May all who are in need of food share in what I am about to enjoy, and may God show me how I may share with others that which they do not have.

4. Before accepting any blessing

Adopt A Code Of Conduct

from the material world (whether purchased with money, obtained through your labor, acquired by exchange, or received as a gift), say mentally: By the privilege of God I receive this, and I pray that it will help me to fulfill my mission in life. This applies even to the receipt of such things as clothing or other personal necessities; an evening of pleasure at the theater or concert hall; a sense of inner peace experienced while in a church, mosque, synagogue, or temple; small items such as books, pamphlets, or other helpful reading material; and, of course, money (in the form of salary, commission, gifts, to name a few possibilities).

5. Whenever you receive any special blessing, such as material things that you have long desired, or a small or large luxury item, or an unexpected bit of goodness, do not apply it to your own personal use in any way until you have spent a few minutes in silence to meditate

and ask this question: Have I truly deserved this blessing, and is there any way in which I can share the benefit of it—directly or indirectly—with others or for the benefit of humanity? Then wait for an answer from the Cosmic. If you receive no word that it is undeserved, or that it should be shared with or passed on to another, then say: I thank God and the Cosmic for this blessing; may I use it to the glow of my Soul.

6. If any special honor—military, governmental, political, social, or otherwise—is conferred on you, act with the utmost humility, proclaim your unworthiness (for who is truly worthy of all things?), and resolve that it will not make you proud or selfish. Accept the blessing with a prayer of thankfulness, and assert that you are receiving it in the name of those whom it enables you to serve better.

7. Never permit yourself to enter discussions of someone else's religious beliefs, except to point

Adopt A Code Of Conduct

out the soundness, goodness, or possible benefits of certain doctrines and thereby show them the good that exists in their religion. Hold not your religious beliefs as superior. Speak well of them, if need be, and point out how they serve you, but do not create in the minds of others the thought that they are in sin or error because of their beliefs. That religion is best for each, which enables him or her to understand God and God's mysterious ways.

8. Be tolerant on all subjects, and bear in mind that destructive criticism creates nothing but sorrow. Unless you can offer constructive criticism, refrain from speaking altogether.

9. Attempt no direct reforms in the lives of others. Discover in yourself what needs correction and improve yourself, so that by the Light of your Life you may help point the way for others.

10. Flaunt not your achievements; do not boast of your code of con

duct. You may be a very upright and well-disciplined person, and by virtue of being in full control of your life, you may possess tremendous knowledge and power, but keep in mind that even the greatest and highest among us is but a child of knowledge[1] and is unworthy of worldly recognition. Proclaim yourself not as a master but as a student, eternally.

11. Seek to share what you can spare, daily, even if in small ways or in meager amounts. Go out of your way to find out where the services you are capable of providing, or the money or material things you can afford to give, would truly be a blessing to the needy. While performing this duty, shun all personal glows and let it be known that you are simply "about the work of the Cosmic."

12. Accept no personal thanks for any blessings you bestow, any gift you give, or any help you render. When thanks are expressed, make a point of saying

Adopt A Code
Of Conduct

the following: Please thank me not, for it is I who am grateful. I seek, and must seek, to serve and labor for the Cosmic; you have afforded me an opportunity. Now the obligation to pass it on rests with you; may you, too, find an opportunity to serve someone else. (You could use any other words you feel comfortable with to convey the same message.)

13. Accept no gift of a material nature for any good you do unless you intend to donate it to charity. At the moment of accepting it, inform the giver that you will divide the blessing with someone else, so that it will continue to carry on its mission of relief and help. This is especially important when the material gift is of such a nature as money, food, or clothing that can be divided and is a common necessity on the part of many.

14. Bear in mind that as you give, so shall you receive. As each opportunity to give is seized upon with the utmost impulsiveness,

so will future blessings, sought or required, be granted to you by the Cosmic. The greater the degree of impulsiveness — with little thought as to personal sacrifice — the greater will be the compensation credited in the Cosmic.

15. Respect all persons; honor thy father and mother; be sympathetic to the sinful, helpful to the afflicted, and of service to the Cosmic. He is greatest among you who is the greatest servant unto all.

16. Go to the assistance of any living being, regardless of race, creed, or color, when you can render direct or indirect aid in any emergency. If you cannot give aid in person but can make a telephone call or solicit aid, this, too, is important. In quiet and peace perform your work, render your service, and retire with as little recognition as possible.

17. Maintain one place in your home that is sacred to you, and

Adopt A Code
Of Conduct

use it to find peace and quiet time for daily meditation. Profane it not with unholy acts of the flesh, but sanctify it with your higher thoughts.

18. Give your support, moral or physical, to some church, mosque, temple, or synagogue in your community, so that it may have your help in carrying on its Great Mission.

19. Judge not, unless you are so placed that those to be judged come legally and formally before you in your capacity as an accredited adjudicator of the law, or as a civil servant, or, in some cultures, as a respected community leader. Then in sympathy, understand; in mercy, comprehend; in leniency, estimate; and with love, be fair. For the Law of Compensation will make adequate demands, and the God of all is alone a truly competent judge of all facts.

20. Repeat no slander, tell no tales, and support no reports that injure or condemn, unless accompanied by at least an equal measure of constructive criticism and comment—and then only after you have completely investigated and learned all the facts.

21. Seek the good in all things and give public praise to what you find. Look not upon the changing character of the outer self, but discover the real Self within. Learn to know all beings and love them.

22. Gamble not with the lot of another who, in ignorance, stands to lose or suffer whatever you may gain.

23. Avoid all extremes of thought and action; be moderate in all desires, and subdue your passions in all directions.

24. Attempt no radical or sudden changes in the natural scheme of things; remember the age-old injunction, Not by revolution, but through evolution, are all things accomplished in permanency.

Adopt A Code
Of Conduct

25.   Hold sacred, and above all criticism, your high moral ideals. Permit no slander to affect the good name you have made for yourself. Live that life which will prove the goodness of your principles. In short, live by example; practice what you preach.

---

1. *A child of knowledge means nobody knows it all. We all learn new things everyday like a child.*

CHAPTER 13
Take Time to Relax and Commune with Nature

Contrary to the Laws of Nature, we human beings have evolved a custom of living not as originally decreed in the divine scheme of things but, in many ways, as decried by nature and abhorred by divine principles. We have removed ourselves from the

Take Time To Relax And Commune With Nature

open country and avoided contact with the natural forces of the earth: the sunlight, the earth's magnetism, the fresh vegetation, the pure water, and the proper cosmic vibrations. Instead, we confine ourselves in small enclosures, in foul air, in darkness, and in the breeding places of disease, germs, and ill-health, all in the name of so-called "civilization."

We continually set aside the right of the body to have freedom of expression, unimpaired freedom of movement, and proper ease. Instead, we tighten around our bodies various limiting and binding articles of clothing. We put pressure on the vessels and nerves of our bodies, bind our feet, throw our bodies out of balance in walking or standing, and generally treat our bodies in a manner that is contrary to the laws of nature.

We ignore the need for rest and sleep. We negate the demands of the functioning organs, and arbitrarily adopt "schedules" for them which are inconsistent with the rhythms of nature. In a myriad of ways, we force our physical growth and our physical development into patterns that are not in harmony with the dictates of nature.

Nature has provided us with the elements we need for the nourishment and maintenance of our body from day to day, yet we arbitrarily select but a few of these and abstain from the rest. In our thoughts and actions, we frequently violate some law of nature for which we must pay the penalty in the form of pain and suffering, disease, and ill health. Only in normal, healthy bodies can our souls function in an optimum manner. If we are to find God, happiness, success, and prosperity in life, we must maintain our bodies in a way that manifests the divine. If we allow the physical framework to deteriorate, we weaken the ability of our souls — the very essence of our being — to function in all their majesty and power.

There is no question about the fundamental principles involved. We need to get back to nature! We need to get back to nature's way of living! We need to get back to the earth! We need to get into the sunshine and enjoy the vegetation and the minerals that nature has provided for our health and well being. We need to take in fresh air, expand our consciousness, and give greater freedom to our divinity to express itself.

You may ask, How can I do all of this? Well, I'm so glad you asked! The answer is as follows:

Get out into the open country, and remember that there are certain natural laws, which you can exploit to promote your health and to benefit yourself in many ways. Don't lose sight of the fact that while there is vitality and life in the air you breathe, this vitality is only a complement to another brand of vitality that is necessary for perfect health. This other vitality comes from the earth itself.

We are living on Planet Earth, which is like a huge magnet. The magnetism of Earth is as essential to our health as is the air we breathe. We have gradually been isolating ourselves from a full enjoyment of this earthly magnetism, by adopting different ways of clothing our bodies, and especially in wearing shoes and other things that separate us or isolate us from the earth's magnetism. Very few people seem to realize that the wearing of shoes is one of the greatest detriments to the mainte

Take Time To Relax And Commune With Nature

nance of perfect health.

The German natural scientist who promulgated the notion of removing one's shoes and taking a walk barefooted for an hour a day was revealing an ancient, fundamental truth. He advocated walking in the early-morning dew in order that this rich, magnetic water might come in contact with the flesh of the body. Most certainly, dew water has magnetism in it that the stale water of reservoirs never contains. There is a good reason why the children of past times found so much pleasure in the old swimming hole. The vitality of that water charged with the earth's magnetism was a veritable stimulant for them; it filled them with more pep and vitality than anything that could have been given to them in the form of food or nourishment.

When you go out in the country, try to choose a place where you can easily take off your shoes and stockings and walk barefooted, even if only in the sunshine on the dry grass. If you can wade in a brook or other body of fresh running water, be sure to do so at least once a day, and take advantage of the morning dew every day that you're there. If you can bathe in some running stream, take along a bathing suit and get the utmost benefit from the wonderful treat of nature.

Drink plenty of water that comes through living wells instead of reservoir water, and drink it as often each day as you possibly can. Eat plenty of fruit and, after every meal, lie down on the grass or the ground in the shade and sleep. Bask in the sunlight each day while lying on the ground, so that your body absorbs the magnetic conditions of both great polarities: the earth and the sun.

Do not overlook the fresh, green vegetables. Try to eat as many of these raw as you possibly can. Remember that cooking or boiling vegetables extracts the important juices, and that these are often cast away with the water. Hunt for some fresh dandelion and watercress, and eat some of these before each meal, after properly washing them. Eat plenty of asparagus, celery, lettuce, spinach, turnips, and carrots. Green peas, lima beans, and many other vegetables, such as carrots, can be eaten raw with great benefit.

Do not spend your vacation at a place where you have to change clothes several times a day in order to compete with others who may be there solely for that purpose. Get back to nature in every sense of the word, and wear clothing that is as simple and loose about your body as possible. Do not mind how much dirt you get on your body or into your system. Go to sleep clean each night with plenty of fresh air, lying flat on your back in bed if possible, and never mind how soiled or disheveled you may become during the day. Take along some books on subject matter that is likely to constitute the basis of new thoughts, new ideas, and new principles in your life. Make the vacation period a time for physical, mental, and spiritual regeneration.

Plan your vacation with a view to sharing it, if you can, with someone who is less fortunate than you—for example, it could be an elderly person, a child, or a neighbor. If necessary, cut down your two-week vacation to only one week, and take that person with you for that week. You will find that you create in the Cosmic Realm, a richer life and more blessings for yourself.

CHAPTER 14

Epilogue

Dear reader, congratulations for making it to this section of the book. Hopefully, you have read and disseminated all the ideas and concepts espoused in this book. The taste of the pudding, as they say, is in the eating. Practice makes perfect. So, it is up to you to take control of your life by practicing all you have read in this book as best you can. If you do, you will surely reap the benefits. The following paragraphs attempt to capsulize the essence of this book. If you have truly read and understood this book, most of the following discourse would sound familiar to you. If you have not yet read the book in its entirety, these paragraphs would also serve as an introduction to what to expect in the book. So, either way, you will benefit from reading this section of the book.

TAKE CONTROL OF YOUR LIFE

In one of the ancient temples, built for worship in solitude and silence, there appears over the portals this inscription: "Man, know thyself: Know then thyself, presume not God to scan; the proper study of mankind is MAN." Mysticism, as known throughout the ages, involves the intimate and direct awareness of God or the Cosmic through self. To know yourself, then, is to know God, for God is literally within. The journey which leads us to that ultimate experience is the Mystical Awakening.

Through our various faith beliefs, we have come to know that the summum bonum, the supreme or highest good, is God or Being. God is omnipotent, omnipresent, and omniscient: the All, the Absolute. God is everywhere present, being the past, present, and the future all in one. Nothing exists outside of God, for God is infinite in time as well as in space. To being there cannot be a state of non-being. God is both substance and the faculty of awareness of its substance. God is not evolving, for God is perfect already. In finite terms, everything that has been, exists now; or will be, already exists within Being. Nothing is God, but God is everything.

In the words of ancient philosophers: "To Being there has never been a beginning, for nothing cannot give rise to something." Thus, we have always existed as spiritual beings, the children of God. Each one of us is a soul personality, an unseparated segment of the Universal Soul of God. As soul personalities, we were given minds with which to think and reason, wills with which to choose, and access to the one great force and

Epilogue

intelligence pervading all. As sons and daughters of God we are literally God incarnate with all the power that is implied.

What stands between us, then, and health, happiness, success, self-mastery, or essential goodness? From the beginning it has been self, the ego, that has been the undoing and downfall of humanity, and it is only through self that we may regain our status. Through our own free will and reason, we either adhere to or contradict Divine Law. Nothing separates us from the realizations of the Divine Unity but ourselves. Not until we choose to know the Cosmic or Natural Laws does God show us the path. In the words of the Lord Jesus Christ (for those of the Christian faith): "Ask, and it shall be given you; seek, and ye shall find; knock, and it shall be opened unto you: For every one that asketh, receiveth; and he that seeketh, findeth; and to him that knocketh, it shall be opened."

But there also exists the corollary: "Ask not, and it shall not be given you; seek not, and ye shall not find; knock not, and it shall not be opened unto you." Our destiny is of our own making; we create our future, consciously or unconsciously, by our every thought and act.

As sons and daughters of God, we are not only thinking, reasoning, rational beings but we are also emotional, psychic beings. As we think and reason, we create urges and desires-and desires call forth emotions. Emotions move us to action, and then we are compelled to make a choice between the desires of the moment. This choice, the exercising of our will, is toward the desire that our thinking and reasoning has determined to be good and beautiful and is usually the strongest desire of the moment. If our thinking and reasoning is positive and in accordance with the will of God, we will create happiness or harmony in our lives. If, however, our thinking and reasoning has been negative, we will create in our lives disharmony, pain, and suffering. The gift of life itself and of consciousness constitutes the greatest blessing that God and the Cosmic can bestow upon a human being. All of the Cosmic operates in harmony and with vibrations that harmonize in all departments of life. We cannot break cosmic laws, but we can become out of harmony with them. It is when we are out of harmony with Being or God that we suffer and become sick and unhappy. Most of the unhappiness in this world, however, is due to our own ignorance of the divine nature of the inner or psychic self and the creative power of thought.

People who seek to solve their problems by escape or by looking for the cause outside themselves or for a greater power outside themselves are only fooling themselves and adding to their own problems and unhappiness. There is no greater master than the Master Within. The soul of humanity has thus been brought here to see the words of God made manifest, for there is literally an unseparated segment of God residing within each of us.

The psychic body, invisible to most, recognized by a few, is the Divine Power, the only power that humanity possesses. It is the inherent nature of a human being, and in fact all of Being, to tend toward imbalance or disharmony. It is through mind that the forces,

Epilogue

which have moved us to an imbalance, are given direction and allow us to achieve once again a state of harmony, only to tend toward imbalance again. This inherent nature of chance, from imbalance to harmony and back again, continues in a cyclic fashion as we move from one experience to another.

We are sensitive to the imbalance that occurs within us. It is this sensitivity which creates urges and desires that impel the body and mind to action. Our whole lives are devoted to seeking this ever-elusive state of harmony. Everything that we do, whether consciously or unconsciously performed, is for the purpose of removing disharmony within our life.

We each live in our own self-created illusion world of the mind. Everything that we perceive takes place within our own mind. Our world of reality is not only dependent upon what we have perceived, but our understanding of it as well. Our world is the product of our own creative thinking and, through the creative power of thought, we find in our world exactly what we expect to find whether or not that is what we want to find. We are each responsible for the world we see. We each choose the feelings that we experience and decide the goals that we would achieve. Everything that seems to happen, we have asked for by our thoughts and acts. Life is like a drama, for we ourselves determine what roles we play; whether we are happy or sad; and it is we who write the script.

We have attracted to us those people, places, and situations as a product of our own thoughts. If we find ourselves unhappy or we have failed to achieve that we have desired in our lives, we can blame no one but ourselves. Only we have the power to change them through an understanding and application of the forces and laws of which we are a part.

There is no greater force available to humanity than the creative power of thought. Mind is ever the builder and the way. Remember the adage: "Whatsoever a man sows, that shall he also reap." But we cannot solve life's problems by doing nothing for, alas, there also exists the corollary: "Whatsoever a man fails to sow that shall he also fail to reap."

When the Lord Jesus Christ was asked which is the great commandment in the law, he replied: "Thou shalt love the Lord thy God with all thy heart, and with all thy soul, and with all thy mind." This is the first and great commandment. The second reads, "Thou shalt love thy neighbor as thyself." On these two commandments hang all the laws and the prophets.

Self-mastery, you will find, is not a destination but a continuing journey. The direction in which you are traveling determines success or failure.

Our life is not what others conceive it to be, but what it appears to us to be. The world is such as we conceive it to be. If we would change our conception, we would change the world.

So, where do we start? We start with ourselves. We should take a good look at self; the kind of person we are. We should examine our thoughts and emotions, and we should take a good look at our attitudes and motives in what we think and do. We should start to portray to the world, through our thoughts and acts, the kind of person that we inwardly want to be. You will find that you cannot consistently act in a manner

Epilogue

inconsistent with what you are for, through the creative power of thought, you become the person that you portray to the world.

Remember the adage: "Like begets like." Acts of kindness beget further acts of kindness. Acts of anger beget further acts of anger. If we would receive compassion and love, we must be compassionate and loving. This is a law, not a moral.

You will perhaps learn, also, that it is wrong to judge people by the mistakes they have made but, rather, by the motive that is within their heart. The Cosmic does not weigh or measure the actual size, nature, or quality of a gift or act, but by the intent, purpose, and spirit back of it.

We live in a causative world. For every effect that we see, there is a cause. Likewise, for every act or cause, there is an effect somewhere. To understand the effects we see in our lives and to solve life's problems we must first become aware of the forces within ourselves. It is only when we turn our point of inquiry inward and attempt to know ourself as the great mystery of all mysteries that we come to understand God.

To know self is to know one's heritage and power. It is not sufficient, however, for us to know only ourself, for we must also learn to use ourself. To attain peace and harmony within, we must first understand that self is an integral part of Being. It is only when we become aware of God in all things that an awakening occurs. The key to our happiness can come only after we have come to understand our true relationship to God and to all humanity. We either face toward the light or away from the light--there is no in between. Light is the way of love; darkness is the way of doubt and fear.

Evil exists within God's permissive will but is not expressive of His intentional will. As sons and daughters of God we have been given free will with which to choose. Evil becomes reality when we rebel and choose outside the law of love. The reality of evil lies in our own abuse of the law, prideful motivation, and misguided choices. We can do what we want to do and be what we want to be. There are no limitations on the mind except those that we acknowledge. Remember, the body is the temple of the living God, both as to the place to meet Him and as an instrument through which we may attune to Him.

The purpose of our life is to gain the knowledge from experience that will allow us to comprehend that which is infinite and eternal, and to express the true nature of the inner self: the God Within. With the gaining of the understanding of that which comes from within and its source, there comes the awakening or development of the spiritual entity, and there must follow an attaining of the higher physical, mental, and spiritual balance when the body becomes subservient to the soul, and the soul is as free in matter as out of it.

The earth cycles are complete. The will conforms with the will of God. This is the Ultimate Experience-- to be in control of one's life, thus attaining self-mastery and happiness.

OTHER BOOKS

BY

ROBERT O. OWOLABI

Other Books By Author

Title: AN AFRICAN'S VIEW OF THE AMERICAN SOCIETY: An Eyewitness Account Of Over 15 Years of Living, Studying and Working in the United States of America

ISBN: 1-57087-227-9

Date Published: July 2, 1996

Publisher: Professional Press
Chapel Hill, NC 27515-4371

Contents

Preface

Introduction

Chapter 1	America: God's Own Land
Chapter 2	Life At College
Chapter 3	My Entry Into The American Job Market
Chapter 4	The American Work Ethic
Chapter 5	Opportunities For Americans: Really Equal?
Chapter 6	The Glass Ceiling

An African's View Of The American Society

Chapter 7   Racism In America: The Denial Syndrome

Chapter 8   Americans And Hypocrisy

Chapter 9   Black America As I See It

Chapter 10   The American Justice System

Chapter 11   African-Americans and Africans In America

Chapter 12   Assisting Immigrants To Assimilate: How Well?

Chapter 13   The Xenophobic/Xenophilic Syndrome

Chapter 14   The Day I Became An American Citizen

Chapter 15   The Challenge For The Future

Chapter 16   Creed of Peace

SYNOPSIS

This book is written to present a balanced and unbiased account of my experience in the United States of America. In the process, personal opinions are also expressed in the bid to reflect on my experience.

Other Books By Author

America is obviously a melting-pot of experiences, good, bad, and ugly. By nature of her body politic, America is endowed with the ability to absorb and accommodate all kinds of people with all kinds of persuasions. It appears that is exactly why God allowed America to be founded. Only in America can you be what you want to be, as long as you operate within the limits of the laws of the land. Nobody would be able to stop you, even if some of the things you do or say may be anti-social or anti-establishment. The American system is designed such that you can aspire to be very rich, and, with hard work and some luck, become very rich. The same system can allow you to remain poor, if you so choose. The system will even provide you with necessary level of sustenance to perpetually maintain that level of poverty.

However, if you choose to be middle-class, which majority of Americans are, you will have to work for and maintain that state of existence without much support from the system. While all these opportunities exist for all Americans, the chances of making the best of them may not be equal for all Americans. If you are white, it appears you have all the chances to make the best of the system. If you are other than white, it appears you must strive harder in other to harness the available opportunities to your advantage. The bottom line is that everybody can achieve the "American Dream", if they want to. The road to achieving it may appear more thorny for some than others. It follows the popular saying that "life is not fair." This appears to be the American reality, from my perspective. Every American has different perspectives about this issue.

An African's View Of The American Society

But the perspective always varies proportionately with the life experience of the individual.

A typical white American would be quick to say that if a person works hard and stays out of trouble, they would achieve the American dream and live a comfortable life. However, a typical non-white American would not be that quick to make the same admission because they may have encountered artificial barriers in their quest for societal survival. This bears credence to the saying that "experience is the best teacher," or "the taste of the pudding is in the eating." The purpose of this book is to attempt to provide a reflection on the American society as seen by an outsider looking in. All of the examples given and views expressed are based on my personal experiences and observations since I have been in this country. I hope the content of this book will serve as another mirror through which America can see herself as she is being seen from the outside.

Other Books By Author

Title: EFFECTIVE PARENTING: Strategies That Work And Mistakes To Avoid

ISBN: 0-9666450-0-6

Date Published: May 1, 1999

Publisher: Bob & Bob Publishing Gaithersburg, MD, 20898-0246

CONTENTS

Preface

Introduction

Chapter 1   Who Is A Parent?

Chapter 2   Basic Responsibilities Of A Parent

Chapter 3   Parental Authority

Chapter 4   Do Children Have Rights?

Chapter 5   Should Respect Be Reciprocal Between Parent And Child?

Chapter 6   Discipline In The Home

Chapter 7   The Guilt Factor

Effective Parenting

Chapter 8 — Community Role In Parenting

Chapter 9 — When Does A Child Outgrow Discipline?

Chapter 10 — When Does A Child Become An Adult?

Chapter 11 — Parenting Teenagers

Chapter 12 — Sibling Rivalry: What Can Parents Do?

Chapter 13 — Case Studies

Chapter 14 — Reflections

Chapter 15 — Life's A Trip

SYNOPSIS

This book sets out to establish guidelines for effective parenting. The guidelines are not based on any academic research or religious doctrine or dogma. They are based primarily on the experience of the author. After all, experience, the sages say, is the best teacher! Some lessons are also borrowed from tradition, reason and pure common sense. Some expert opinions (albeit esoteric), contemporary and pragmatic, were also drawn from. An attempt was made to cover examples of children of all age groups but the book is definitely not a 'be-all' or 'end-all' on parenting.

Other Books By Author

Parenting, being a life-long endeavor, has so many facets to it that it poses a big challenge to cover all aspects of it in a book of this nature. However, there is definitely enough material for any parent, whether seasoned or just beginning, to draw from and use as appropriate. Some chapters even include 'rules' that could guide parents to make informed decisions, or act appropriately under various circumstances.

Parenting is a sacred duty ordained by God, Allah, Yahweh, the Cosmic, or the Universal Soul Essence, depending on the individual's belief system. Hence, no amount of education or reading can make one a perfect parent, unless one first strives to attain perfect communion with God Almighty, Allah, Yahweh, the Cosmic, the Universal Soul Essence, or the god of one's heart. In short, the sacredness of such a secular art, makes it incomplete if one attempts to undertake it purely through intellectual understanding without divine guidance or intervention. The interjection of 'divine guidance' here has nothing to do with religion. It is only an acknowledgment of the supernatural or superhuman elements of the art of parenting in the true sense of it! Translation: No parent can do it alone! It requires a combination of the parents' good and appropriate intentions, divine intervention and community cooperation, for a parent to undertake the unique art of effective parenting.

Order Form

Fax orders: (301) 990-2393

Telephone orders: (301) 977-3442

E-mail orders: bobandbobinc@aol.com
On-line orders: http://www.bobandbob.com
http://www.amazon.com
http://www.barnesandnoble.com
http://www.borders.com
Postal Orders: Bob & Bob Associates, Inc., P.O. Box 10246, Gaithersburg, MD 20898-0246

Please send the following book(s) by Robert O. Owolabi:
<u>**An African's View of The American Society**</u> **$11.95**
<u>**Effective Parenting**</u> **$4.95**
<u>**Take Control of Your Life**</u> **$9.95**

I understand that I may return the book(s) for a full refund—for any reason, no questions asked.

Company Name: _____

Name: _____

Address: _____

City: _____ State: _____ Zip: _____ - _____

Telephone: (____) _____

Shipping and Handling: FREE!!!

Payment: Check or Money Order (*Made payable to: Bob & Bob Associates, Inc.*). Mail your order to the address shown above. Total enclosed: $_____

Order Form

Fax orders: (301) 990-2393

Telephone orders: (301) 977-3442

E-mail orders: bobandbobinc@aol.com
On-line orders: http://www.bobandbob.com
http://www.amazon.com
http://www.barnesandnoble.com
http://www.borders.com

Postal Orders: Bob & Bob Associates, Inc., P.O. Box 10246, Gaithersburg, MD 20898-0246

Please send the following book(s) by Robert O. Owolabi:

An African's View of The American Society	**$11.95**
Effective Parenting	**$4.95**
Take Control of Your Life	**$9.95**

I understand that I may return the book(s) for a full refund—for any reason, no questions asked.

Company Name: _____

Name: _____

Address: _____

City: _____ State: ____ Zip: _____-____

Telephone: (____) _____

Shipping and Handling: FREE!!!

Payment: Check or Money Order (*Made payable to: Bob & Bob Associates, Inc.*). Mail your order to the address shown above. Total enclosed: $_____